Jaime A. Pineda, Ph.D.

PIERCING THE CLOUD:
ENCOUNTERING THE REAL ME

A Life Review

Publisher:

BookBaby 7905 N. Crescent Blvd. Pennsauken, NJ 08110

ISBN: 978-1-09832-407-0 eBook ISBN: 978-1-09832-408-7

Printed in the United States of America. First Edition.

The Mythology of Me
—J. A. Pineda
(With apologies to Albert Camus)

In that split second
When furtively glancing back
At a lived life,
And contemplating
The underlying commonality
Of actions taken,
Has created this unique moment.
It becomes incontrovertible
That something other than me
Is the guiding force.
Convinced of the extra-ordinary origin
Of all that is me,
The universe becomes
Personal,
Precious,
Poignant,
Pregnant
With possibilities,
Producing a big-bang.
It is a happy moment!

OTHER BOOKS BY THE AUTHOR:

Mirror Neuron Systems:
The Role of Mirroring Processes in Social Cognition. Humana Press, 2009.

Book of Verse: The Quieting of a Mind. AuthorHouse, 2017.

The Dawning of a New Mind: Book of Verse II. AuthorHouse, 2019.

C O N T E N T S

PROLOGUE

What motivates someone to write a life review? And why is a life review different from an autobiography? If one is famous or larger than life like say a Churchill, an Einstein, or a Picasso, then such a life review would make sense. Most of us have not discovered the cure for cancer or diabetes, or scored more points in basketball, soccer, hockey, or cricket than anyone, or trekked through all the five continents on Earth. The lack of identifiable achievements might limit the story and the motivation to talk of one's life. So, why write the story? Why the desire to share what one has experienced? The answer is as clear and simple to me as the warbling of a bird in spring.

Life is a transformation, and the vicissitudes of unique experiences transformed my life, just like everyone else's. We all have interesting lives and have something to say to affect others. As Lee Gutkind, the godfather of creative nonfiction, says in his book *You Can't Make this Stuff Up*, "We write to say something that matters, to have an impact on society, to put a personal stamp on history." Deep in my heart, I hear a melody resonating with all of existence and sharing it is an imperative. My individual story matters less than the revelation of a greater awareness of which we are all part. It is this greater nature of being that motivates this story, so everyone can see themselves in it and identify with that reality. There is, then, a metaphysical aspect in this life review. When the Buddha was asked metaphysical questions, he typically maintained silence, as such questions are answered only individually and personally. I write my story consciously aware of this fact, hoping that you, the reader, will not view my experience as being the ultimate answer to such questions but as a collection of personalized experiences that are meant to motivate you to find your own unique answers.

INTRODUCTION

I call this a life review rather than an autobiography because it is more than just my individual story. A major goal is to understand the meaning of my life within the context of this larger existence. It is, therefore, an attempt to hear not the individual events or notes as historical facts, but as a tune in a much larger symphony. A life review is what everyone should attempt to do to discover their own unique melody and significance.

My individual story relates to change, both large and small. Expected and unexpected. Continuous and discontinuous. And even transcendent changes in circumstances, and personal transformations that interacted with my biological predispositions to make me who I am. How all these changes came together, whether planned and inevitable or spontaneous and unpredictable, is the great mystery. But come together they did in unusual and interesting ways.

From the perspective of such a retrospective, my life provides hints regarding these changes and their meaning. Hence, one strong motivation for writing a life review involves the search for meaning. Only in reviewing my life have trends and patterns emerged, pointing to such things. Actions, playing roles, and stories defining my personality characterized my childhood, adolescence, and early adulthood. As a poignant example, the rewarding nature of playing the part of the good son, a good student, and an obedient and loving family member became clear to me early on. I solidified these roles as parents, family, friends, and teachers reinforced them.

When I turned nine, my life transformed. It was the beginning of a new and different me. What made this new life possible was detachment from my immediate family, my friends, the environment I knew and loved, my culture, and my native language. Circumstances forced me to let go of everything known and meaningful to me. Rather than being traumatized by the experience, it led me to recognize how many of the stories defining my "self" were more made-up than real. The search for meaning and identity during my childhood and adolescence motivated the need to create stories. Feeling a psychological emptiness, my overactive imagination quickly filled the gap. This is what all humans do. Over the years, I have realized that the emptiness we all may sense at certain times in our lives is in fact not emptiness at all but filled with something I could neither sense nor understand. What I now realize is that who I am has been complete from the beginning, and the need to make up stories to fill a nonexistent emptiness was both unnecessary and counterproductive. Along with the reinforcement provided by parents, siblings, friends, and strangers, the stories gained a solidity and a reality to them.

When I turned twenty-five, a friend offered to do a numerology reading for me. I have kept his analysis because the prediction of events from the year of my birth until 2016, the last year mentioned, has been a source of fascination and entertainment, for it has been eerily accurate. The most intriguing part concerns its description of the basic motivating force behind all my actions. It says: "You like order in everything." In reviewing my life, one peculiar recurring theme stands out—my sensitivity to and need for order. From such a predisposition, others might have predicted I would become a scientist, although science seemed the least likely scenario I would have considered in my early twenties. These and other such details from the numerology analysis highlight at least one important metaphysical question: How can a complex life, full of infinite decisions and possibilities not yet expressed, be so predictable. So transparent? Is it a coincidence. Or, are there forces beyond our comprehension playing a large and meaningful role in our lives?

As an adult with a more mature intellect and aspiration, my effort turned to exploring and understanding the "mythologies of me," my personally created stories. Through such an understanding, I hoped to recognize my real and true nature and live from such an awareness. This realization did not mean I wanted to forget false or incomplete memories, rather it meant exploring them to get closer to the underlying kernel of truth. Having such an understanding is how I have examined my memories. As a neuroscientist, I now recognize memories as present-moment recreations of past events that change from the original experience. This is one reason creative nonfiction is the name for this genre of writing. For while it aims to be truthful, it is a varying personal perception of this truth. The questions resonating after many years of such an inquiry are: Why do "I" exist as an individual? Is there a role for me in life? Is what "I" do important? How does my story relate to others? How does it relate to the larger story of life? Are these even worthwhile questions to ask?

More than anything, my life and this life review have convinced me of a greater intelligence or presence guiding my growth and development from the beginning. Perhaps unusual, unexpected, or transformative events might occur once, twice, or even thrice in one's lifetime and still be coincidences. But when similar encounters occur over and over and over, one's natural skepticism dissolves and we must consider alternative explanations. To understand this and answer the question of my significance and meaningfulness, I had to first know who and what I am. From such a perspective, doing a life review is a kind of psychological and spiritual requirement.

There are several small undercurrents relevant to writing this life review. First, as a scientist, organizing my life on paper is satisfying, for the process has allowed me to detect patterns in a life, which, like in all lives, make a messy set of data points. Searching for patterns in this immense array of events is the essential *raison d'être* of scientific research and my vocation. Second, as a teacher, I want to help others. I see my story as an opportunity to share my personal, scientific, and spiritual lessons learned over a lifetime. Third, as a human being, a life review comprises some selfish and narcissistic components. In the back of my mind is the idea that no one knows my story, and I want to share it to experience validation for my life. Whether contemporaries read my story is not as important as some future reader, an anthropologist, or a curious soul, who recognizes the story for the gift I mean it to be (I said narcissistic, right?), discovers and reads it. Finally, writing with six-and-a-half decades of living behind me and a bit of living still ahead of me, I wanted to develop a skeletal outline of my most memorable experiences, before those memories fade. By placing such memories in a narrative story style, I could then remember and review them, similar to examining old photographs with a story line or watching a video. I have added more and more detail as one memory primed others, and as the narrative grew, so did new reasons for completing it. Still, the story remains a skeletal outline, with compressed and recreated scenes and dialog, for such a narrative cannot fully capture all the nuances and details of a lived life. I hope that readers of this life review can discover in my story a bit of their own, for what I am, you are, and what happened to me, can happen to anyone.

PART I

SEARCH FOR MEANING

CHAPTER ONE
Personal Big Bang

What does "attuned to life" mean?
It is a state of heightened awareness,
To the life forces all around.
A feeling of overwhelming love for everything and everyone.
It is, at its roots, an identification with life.

A. A Positive, Creative Force

At four years of age, I got hold of a slingshot. I went to the front yard of our house, put a small stone in it, and pulled the rubber bands back as far as I could. I then aimed the slingshot toward a fluttering hummingbird approximately 30 yards away. What happened next has haunted me for sixty-two years. When I released the stone, I saw the small, roundish object almost in slow motion hit the hummingbird and the small bird dropped to the ground dead. A moment of shock followed. Why this small incident had such relevance to me was puzzling for many years. Then one day while reviewing the incident, I understood how in a split second and without malicious intent, I had killed a wondrous and living being. The event previewed a possibility of a life that could have been my reality.

Fortunately, I did not grow up to be a destructive force, except for the occasional temper tantrums. In fact, I became the antithesis of destruction, what I optimistically characterize as a positive, creative force. Rebelliousness, a milder form of destructiveness, manifested itself in my siblings, but it did not in me, even though I secretly wished for it. Truth is, the qualities more natural to me were a quietness and reserved persona. My introverted quality reflected a curiosity and sensitivity to external events, like the death of a small bird. Despite my quietness, however, I did not see myself as shy until I associated it with fear, low self-esteem, and meekness. My childhood and adolescent personality reflected confidence, not the boasting type of confidence but a quiet confidence reflected in my actions and speech. My friends often saw me as a leader.

I was born on the thirteenth day of the sixth month of the year, and in our society, we associate the number "13" with bad luck. In fact, the fear of the number 13 has a specific recognized phobia: triskaidekaphobia. Ever since I can recall, I recoiled from such an idea, for the opposite has been true for me. In fact, I have considered myself a lucky person. Not lucky in the sense of inheriting money, rather, lucky in a fated, protective way. For I have always experienced an external mysterious force protecting me from injury and guiding me down a particular path. I encountered this mysterious power early on and especially during critical, opportune, and unexpected moments throughout my life.

Me at two years of age. Nora is in the background

B. In the Right Place and Time

My personal big bang, or birth, occurred in a small town in the middle of a poor Central American country where donkeys were as common as inhabitants. In fact, they refer to those born in my town as donkeys. I assume it's meant to paint us as stubborn creatures. Central America means different things to different people, but to me it is the small land bridge connecting North America and Mexico to South America. In this smallest of central land bridges, seven countries developed, with a total population of about forty-two million people. Honduras is in the middle of this bridge and surrounded by the Caribbean Sea to the north, Guatemala and Belize to the northwest, El Salvador to the southwest, and Nicaragua, Costa Rica, and Panama to its south.

My birth did not happen at a hospital or clinic but at my parent's home in Comayagua, Honduras, on June 13, 1953. Comayagua, the donkey center, is itself found in the middle of the country. In 1953, my parents lived in an old Spanish colonial-style house with two-feet-thick adobe walls, white stucco, red tile roof, dirt floors, and the smell of history for no one knew its true age. A literally cool (heat-wise) house, it stood in a small square along with the second biggest Catholic Church in town. My aunt Maria Luisa, the oldest of Mom's four sisters, was the midwife and made sure the birth transpired without problems. Mom considered my birth the easiest one she had. She did not realize this would be a gift to make up for what would be, in the near future, her experience of a painful letting go. For when I turned nine, my parents would send me off to another country.

Comayagua Cathedral and Town Square

The town of Comayagua wears its long history nonchalantly. Founded in 1537 by Spanish conquistadores on the banks of the Humuya River, it served as the capital of Honduras from 1540 until 1880. Because of its importance, the town has historical and striking Spanish colonial–style buildings, with the largest being the Spanish baroque Catholic cathedral completed in 1715. The cathedral, with its white, thick walls and bell tower overlooking the central square, still serves as the center for all major events. The cathedral loomed large in my childhood, as the center for all the Independence Day, Easter, and Christmas parades my siblings and I took part in. It was also the focus of the weekly Sunday masses my family attended regularly. As the focal point of my baptism, and those of my sisters and brothers, the church held in its archives the records of our religious purification and admission to membership in the Catholic Church. Everyone belonged to the church.

The thought of Comayagua, my hometown, brings back joyful memories of playful things with a serious purpose. On the outskirts of town, the Spaniards built several churches in the sixteenth-century, and a university, the first in Central America. Classes at this university started in 1632, making Comayagua a center of learning while the colonization of Jamestown, Virginia, had barely started in the United States in 1607.

Because these buildings, many now in ruins, occupy hills overlooking the town, they serve as playgrounds and social gathering places for the townsfolk. There is a lot of laughter and friendliness associated with these places. Of greater relevance to me and my friends, the air currents created by the low-lying hills served as perfect places for dads and sons to fly kites. At certain times of the year, given the wind gusts, the urge to go to these hills and fly kites was overwhelming.

When I remember Comayagua, my mind runs down one such hill holding on to a long string, at the end of which is a large kite with a long tail which Dad and I made. I see Dad holding the kite high in the air and then letting it go. The feeling of holding on to the string while the kite goes higher and higher and Dad shouting instructions is both heart-warming and thrilling. Even more special is when the kite, at the zenith of the length of string and lazily swaying in the wind, becomes my connection to Heaven. I take small pieces of paper, write messages on them, attach them to the string, and then fly them up to the kite, one at a time. They are messages to the Divine and speak of gratitude and requests for favors: *Thank you for making Uncle Mario better*; *Please make sure I get that gun for my birthday*; *Please let Letti know that I like her*. I could communicate with the Divine directly and that connection and communion is real. Flying a kite never had a more serious purpose.

By the 1950s, Comayagua, following the move of the capital to Tegucigalpa, had the aura of an abandoned, small, and dusty town. It suffered damage from earthquakes and several fires. Its moribund spirit was rooted in the unpaved, rutted streets and slow-moving carts drawn by oxen. The same slow-moving and carefree cadence reverberated in its citizenry, who seemed not to have a care in the world. Even with a child's body and energy, the same slow rhythms of the town pervaded my body for I was never in a hurry. Time seemed static and never-ending and I saw no need to rush. The only significant daily activity involved getting together with friends to play soccer, everyone's passion that not even school could overshadow.

Despite the tired visage and character of the town, the soil all around the valley was fertile and rich in nutrients conveying the sense of a place with immense possibilities. Settlers had located Comayagua in the most potentially bountiful area of the country. The valley, flat as a pancake, looked up to tall mountains covered with pine tree groves, while rivers crisscrossed it. Rivers that produced the rich, dark soil cuddling its latent fertility, like a mother holding tightly to a child in swaddling clothes waiting for it to grow. As kids, we used the rivers as a playground and the swimming holes for relief from the hot sun. Adults used the river banks as picnic areas to enjoy Sunday afternoons with the whole family.

I emerged from this serene and placid atmosphere, born the second child to middle-class parents, Jaime and Marietta Pineda-Rodriguez. Like the valley itself, I came into the world with the potential to be much more. As tradition would have it, Dad's paternal name became my last name. "Pineda," the stories went, came from our distant Sicilian background, likely originating from the word "pineta" or "pinetum" meaning a grove of pine trees. The coincidence of the name and birthplace setting (Comayagua was surrounded by pine groves) gave me the sense of being born in the right place and right time.

Dad

C. Family Legacy

I inherited many things from Dad, including his open, fierce, and sincere spirit. As one of four brothers (Julio, Jose, Gustavo, Jaime), Dad, a lawyer by trade, developed into a hard-working criminal attorney and became a judge in the small town of Comayagua. His dealings with criminals, many of whom he sent to jail, obliged him to own and carry a gun for protection. The rationale he gave considered police as nonexistent and corrupt. Townsfolk could not depend on them.

One hot summer day while crossing the street to go to work, Dad saw a large, gruff man whom he had sentenced to jail a few years back coming toward him. The look of recognition on the man's face instinctively caused Dad to put his right hand nervously on the pistol he carried under his suit. "I got ready to defend myself and shoot him if I had to," he would say in his deep, resonant voice. Unexpectedly, the man approached with a warm smile and shook Dad's hand.

"Thank you Abogado Pineda," he said, using the Spanish equivalent for Esquire. "You did me a great favor five years ago by sending me to prison," he continued. "It gave me time to rethink my life, and I owe you a great deal for my life is now so much better."

Dad could only smile uneasily. Crossing paths with criminals described a common occurrence for a judge, and the incidents could have gone either way. Fortunately, Dad never used the pistol. His kindness and humility served him better at disarming others—a lesson not lost on me.

It became a moment of pride for the family when Dad reached the pinnacle of his professional career and was named Associate Justice of the Honduran Supreme Court, a role he performed for many years. The event transpired as a nonevent for me since youth and naiveté prevented me from appreciating its significance. I learned that his colleagues deeply admired him as an honest, patriotic, and brilliant attorney, and as a person they could trust. I grew to appreciate his stature even more when his name came up for consideration as Chief Justice. But, as luck would have it, politics stymied those efforts. The accusations brought by his political enemies, which were many, revolved primarily around Dad's origins.

"What makes a real Honduran?" they asked rhetorically. Then, they answered their own question that Dad could not be one even though born in the country. His mother, Grandma Livia, a native of neighboring Nicaragua, had emigrated to Honduras to start the family. Being 100% and a multi-generational Honduran became a prerequisite for the Chief Justice job. In this rough-and-tumble political climate, Dad did not get the job. The decision produced a gloominess in everyone, except him. When I reflect on this, I remember the spirit and grace with which he accepted the decision. He did not react with bitterness or anger. He continued to do his job as he had always done it, in the best way he could.

Dad's spirit lives in me, as I mirror many of his mannerisms, traits, and interests. I show his drive to live a curious, intellectual life regulated by a deep faith in God and actions backed by common sense. In his lifetime, Dad became a published author. Two of the monographs derived from his thesis work, and the third, written when in the Supreme Court, covered nullification of legal opinions, an interesting but boring topic for nonlawyers. I received a copy of the latter work as a gift from him and on the inside cover, he wrote: "For my son, Jaime Armando, in remembrance of your Dad. August 18, 1992."

I don't know whether publications such as these are the norm in Honduras. To me, they speak of his tenacity, attention to detail, and willingness to share with others. As a scientist and teacher, I reflect a similar attention to detail, tenacity to explore life, and eagerness to share my knowledge with others. Dad also became fascinated by and explored Catholic theology, reading extensively on the topic. Like him, I developed significant interest in religion and spirituality and have read extensively in those areas.

Uncharacteristically, Dad developed a reputation for jokes he would tell at social gatherings after a few drinks, a sign he had a practical and playful side. One bawdy joke sealed his reputation as a storyteller. The story is about a landowner who finds himself naked and hanging from a chandelier trying to get away from the husband of the lady with whom he had just shared a bed. I don't recall the punchline, but what I recall is his friends literally begging Dad to retell what they had heard many times before. They yearned to experience his performance and the sound effects associated with the telling. Dad could be a performer when he needed to be, as he gesticulated and dramatized the story. As a teacher, I have similar instincts and have called upon my acting skills to make a dry lecture interesting. Perhaps the only trait I didn't inherit is Dad's ability to tell jokes, as I fail miserably at being funny on purpose, even after much practice or drinking.

The most moving description of Dad came at the end of his life in the form of a eulogy written by a colleague. "This man," his friend said in admiration, became the "Honduran Solomon" a "bright torch of the continent," "a wise man, honest citizen, with the heart of a child, and a humility and simplicity so peculiar to him." I read and reread those words, aware of the great honor it is to be known as a wise, Solomon-like individual. Dad has been a role model for how to live my life.

Mom

Mom played the yin to Dad's yang. In Chinese philosophy, yin and yang describe apparently opposite or contrary forces that are complementary, interconnected, and interdependent in the natural world, and how they may give rise to each other as they interrelate to one another. This perfectly describes Mom and Dad's relationship. She exhibited a vivacious personality and according to her own story married below her social standing, which caused her endless regrets. In Mom, I saw a forceful spirit, good-looking, full of life, who loved us, and cared for the family in the best way she could. Not especially a good cook, she tirelessly prepared meals three times a day. The ever-present dust of a dusty town made every house we lived in a challenge and constant effort to maintain clean. The seven of us who made up her immediate family produced endless amounts of dirty clothes, which she washed by hand since we had no conveniences like a washer and drier.

I remember Mom's smile the most as I watched her do these ordinary things. Most especially, her smile and laughter drew my attention as she talked to her friends in her unique and animated way. Her steadfastness and commitment in her role as wife and mother became teachable traits for all her children. I see in me her sense of joy that she brought to life, coupled with a kind of subtle fierceness and determination. These traits were key to my development and played significant roles in the unfolding nature of my personal and spiritual persona. Her circumstances, unfortunately, eventually overwhelmed her vivacity, *joie de vivre*, and determination as she aged and drifted into a life of sadness and regret. As strong as she seemed, life circumstances proved stronger. She had always aspired for more, but the gradual changes brought on by the inevitability of her circumstance, changed her positive outlook to a more negative one.

Years later, when my parents visited me in the States, my first wife, Liz, understood something different, namely, that my Mom's dissatisfaction with her life situation did not fundamentally revolve around social status. It appeared more of a lack of a satisfying interpersonal relationship with Dad. On that visit, Mom came to Liz one day in a highly distressed emotional state. She seemed desperate to share the source of her sorrow with her and they needed a way to bridge the gap in their language barrier. I was at work so the only available "translator" was an old Spanish/English dictionary we had at home. Liz reached for it and sat down besides Mom, taking turns flipping through the dictionary, searching for just the right word or phrase to convey each other's thoughts. One noun, one adjective, one verb at a time. *Insensitive. Unhelpful. Mute.* Those were the first words Mom identified and shared with Liz. Followed by Liz's "Yes, I understand"

and Mom's corresponding "*ahhh-si! Está bien, entiendo! Exáctamente!*"
And onto the next word they went.

Through this painstaking manner of communication, Mom conveyed how she wished with all her heart that Dad would share his thoughts, his feelings, and his hopes with her regarding his professional career. She desired for him to explain "legalese" to her so she could engage in meaningful conversation with him. She wanted to be treated as an intellectual equal. Likewise, she wanted him to listen and respond to her aspirations and needs. At the very least, Mom wanted Dad to assist with domestic shores. The physical burden of managing a household with all its demands and lack of modern conveniences was wearing on her. She needed help. And she wanted *his* help. But, to have a relationship requires two people who genuinely want to relate. That's what was missing in Mom's world—and likely the void she filled with anxiety and sadness. What's more, Liz remembers how their translate-a-word session ended that day. While expressing how dearly Mom loved me, she also pronounced with conviction that "my son is emotionally just like his father! *Si! Mi hijo es como su padre. Es igual!*" I eventually learned that indeed I had inherited some negative aspects from my Dad.

Mom and her three sisters (Marta, Maria Luisa, and Adriana) and a brother, Mario, claimed to have French and Spanish royal blood, unconfirmed rumors embellishing Mom's attractiveness. In a country where men valued light skin on a woman, she attracted many admirers during her time as a single woman. Lost in the mist of family history and legend is why she chose Dad as her eventual marriage partner. They apparently met and fell in love in the small courthouse in the center of Tegucigalpa, the capital, where he practiced law and she worked as a secretary for a time. I presume his fated sense of going far attracted her. Following their marriage, my parents became part of the social elite of Comayagua: members of the Lions Club, regular church attendees where Dad volunteered to usher, and with many friends who kept their social calendars busy. Social expectations required them to be contributors to the well-being of the town and to the people in it—something they obliged.

From both of my parents, I inherited a sense of social responsibility, especially to others who had less than they did. The lesson repeated itself each time they helped my aunts or uncle with rent payments or doctor bills. Their generosity also extended to strangers, the school I attended, church, and to the town's soccer team. This became clear during one special occasion when Dad, in his early forties and beginning to gain a bit of weight, volunteered to play in a soccer game inaugurating a new stadium. He played as a favor to the town fathers who had requested his involvement to help collect money for payment of the stadium. I remember his trepidation in playing after so many years of inactivity, thinking he would suffer a broken leg or worse.

It was a festive day. The game started while a band played. The crowd shouted and laughed at the old men running up and down the field in shorts and t-shirts. Dad, a defender, stayed back. But then, just before the end of the first half, he stole the ball at midfield. Unexpectedly, he fired a cannon shot with his right foot toward the goalie. Remarkably, the ball netted, and he scored the goal—"un golazo," or a superb goal, as many described it. In a town where soccer ruled and everyone considered themselves an expert, a golazo represented a well-earned compliment. Dad became the talk of the town for the miracle he had created at his age. In his typical way, he put his head down and went to work the following day.

In the family, Dad represented order and Mom the enforcer of that order. In those days, Catholic families were large, with maybe six or more children. Mom was thirty-five years old when she married, an unusually late age for marriage in those days. They had two girls and three boys. Nora was the eldest girl. Followed by me, Jaime II. Then my younger sister, Fatima. My younger brother, Jaime III followed, and then Javier was last. Apparently, my parents loved the name Jaime. To differentiate the boys, my little brother became Jaimito (or little Jaime) and I was recognized by my middle name of Armando or Mando, for short, as most of my friends would call me.

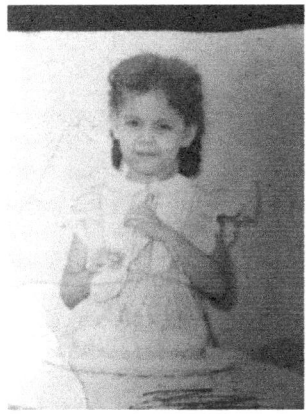

Nora, myself, and Fatima

As the firstborn, my sister Nora was a rebel who made me her special target. Her attractive exterior drew many of the males in the neighborhood—and there were many—yet, good looks concealed a rebellious personality with a bit of a malicious sense of humor. When very young, she played tricks on her younger siblings, namely, me. One such incident occurred when she must have been five years old and I three. Nora asked me to hold a box of matches with two of the matches on either side of the box held down by my thumb and index finger against the striking surface. After instructing me to hold them tightly, she hit the match box hard pushing the small box down onto the floor. Left stuck to my fingers were the two lit matches. I screamed bloody murder.

At times, Nora would sneak up behind me at unpredictable moments and gleefully clobber me on the head and then run off chuckling. I know I didn't merit such torture. But much as I cried and complained, my parents didn't seem concerned and the torment seemed endless. They knew it was what normal siblings did. As a teenager, Nora took up smoking and sometimes stayed out with friends past curfew times. She faced my parents' admonitions and punishment for her rebellious acts, although never seeming to learn her lesson. I envied her a lot, yet could not imitate her since I took the admonitions more seriously.

As the second child, my relationship with Nora and Fatima took different orientations. I reacted to their uniqueness, personalities, and tragedies in distinctive ways. While Nora was older, hostile, aloof, and distant, my younger sister, Fatima, appeared closer, familiar, and more like me. She inherited the best traits of both parents and grew into an obedient and studious child who showed more emotional and outgoing behavior than I did. Because of her more extraverted personality, she had a lot more friends and became more popular, which made me a bit jealous. As an adult, Fatima followed in Dad's footsteps, eventually becoming a lawyer and then a judge. Her career path led her to become closer to him, for she could speak his lawyerly language. Such closeness to Dad, unfortunately, brought her into conflict with Mom, who became jealous of their relationship.

Dad, Mom, and Nora in the back. Fatima, Jaimito, and me in the front.

My little brother Jaimito was almost invisible to me. As the baby in the family, he grew up spoiled. A cute baby and child, he attracted a magnified spotlight from aunts and uncle on anything and everything he did. The intense scrutiny gave way to the development of a lackadaisical attitude, one content with the attention it received. Sweet and humble in spirit, Jaimito showed no interest in school. Several family members speculated he had been born unlucky, or at least uncoordinated, for not a day went by without him accidently bumping his head on something. They speculated this as the reason the poor boy did not do well in school. Once the light of childhood dimmed, and everyone's attention turned elsewhere, Jaimito found himself with a childish dependency on my parents. This dependency slowed his development. He never married, although he fathered a child out of wedlock before he died in his late thirties.

Jaimito admired and looked up to me as his older brother. One summer, when I was sixteen and visiting from the States, he approached me and spoke to me in his sweet and soft twelve-year-old voice. "Can you take me to the States when you return?" he asked. "I don't know what to do here. Maybe I can go with you and help you out."

It was a soulful cry for help and the sadness it elicited made the helplessness it reflected even more poignant. I wasn't sure what to tell him, for as a student I had no means to provide for his support. My lack of an answer and ability to respond made me feel equally helpless. Until his untimely death, I had the luxury of ignoring Jaimito. But his death made real that a brother whom I did not really know had died, and I could never correct that misfortune. Feelings of regret and of lost opportunities engulfed me.

Parents with Javier

The last brother who had a significant impact on my life was Javier. His presence had a profound effect on family dynamics and more point-edly on my career interests. Javier's birth became a possibility when Mom, late in life, began to experience the estrangement of an empty nest and the need to do motherly things.

Javier was born with fine motor skills. He understood language, but did not gain full linguistic communication skills. Like my brother Jaimito, hi verbal deficits made him attached and dependent upon my parents. From the very beginning, the familial bonds between my parents and my two youngest siblings were strong, unusual, and different from those with the older children.

Javier's unusual need for order as a child provided moments of hilarious fun for my young and innocent mind. Once when visiting from the States, I noticed that just before going to bed each night, Javier would arrange his toy soldiers by height—from smallest to largest. More than once and while he slept, I would rearrange the soldiers. I could say the budding scientist in me wanted to conduct an experiment to test his memory and reactions. In reality, my intention had a hint of meanness because I knew my action would trigger an emotional outburst. It never failed. Now, years later, I am convinced that Javier likely suffered from undiagnosed autism spectrum disorder. He died unexpectedly in his twenties in a tragic car accident along with other family members. His life and condition played a key part in my developing career interest in autism.

D. Everyday Life

The family's upward mobility created opportunities and problems. Following my birth in 1953 in the old adobe house, my parents moved to another larger house a block away. The walls of the new house were not as thick, indicating a newer structure. Tiled rather than dirt floors extended throughout the house. It had an inner yard with fruit trees and a semi-large Spanish-style adobe oven.

I can see the house in my mind's eye and happy memories flood my brain, especially birthday celebrations and laughter. In particular, memories spring to mind of Mom's lemonade, horchata, pineapple and other drinks she made of which I could never get enough. A few years after this move, my parents built their own home from scratch on the other side of town. The big move came soon enough, and the family found itself at the edge of town. Because of this, my siblings and I had to walk long distances to school, to the movies, and to the center square where most social events happened. Going to the movies, especially to watch cartoons and Westerns, proved unbearable because of the delays during our walk to the center of town. The adults inevitably would meet an acquaintance and stop to chat, while I twisted and turned waiting for the conversation to end. The movies, all made in Hollywood, projected on the side of the main cathedral, rendered the slow, boring life in Comayagua tolerable for the vividness, the action, and mesmerizing visuals brought to life worlds we only contemplated in our dreams. The stories created unrealistic expectations and dreams of visiting such places that would be untenable for most of us. For me, the movies served as a stimulant for my imagination already in overdrive and I knew I would be the exception.

Living in our new neighborhood meant establishing new friendships and playing roles consistent with our social status. It didn't take long for me to assemble a group of friends who came together to play. Soon, we were the local soccer team. There were the two Hernandez brothers, sons of another lawyer, who lived a few blocks from us and closer to town. The older brother, Roberto, and I competed to be leaders of the group. At least once, we came to physical blows over who would make the rules, assign players to different positions, and decide when and where to play. We were like two young, alpha males fighting over territory.

My parents provided the soccer balls we used and the uniforms for our soccer team. In fact, Mom made the white t-shirts with a blue stripe across the front on her own sewing machine. The design hinted at the Honduran flag, which comprises three horizontal stripes where two are blue and a white one in between. In the middle of the white stripe is a grouping of five blue five-pointed stars in the shape of the letter X. Mom's t-shirt design made the soccer team proud and patriotic. I eventually came to appreciate her big-heartedness. I don't recall being thoughtful and considerate when very young or even aware of such things, including making value judgments regarding most of my friends, except for one.

Pablo stood out. Despite being the same age, he acted much older and wiser than the rest of us. His mannerism and speech exuded humbleness. He walked and talked slower than other kids and lived further out of town—in the sticks. I found out he came from a dirt-poor family. Pablo never wore shoes, yet his calloused feet were a marvel to behold when dribbling the soccer ball. By far the best player on the team, he displayed a level of being, physical prowess, and street smarts beyond our young competencies. I learned a lot watching him. For one, I learned to play better. More central to my story, his cool temperament, wisdom, calmness, and *je ne sais quoi* came to symbolize what I knew I did not have, yet yearned for. I would later associate his personality with a lack of guile and true nature.

Unwritten rules played out differently for folks in the same social milieu. Before moving into the neighborhood, neighbors saw the Hernandez as the family to admire and look up to. They had built a nice brick house, with bars on the windows, and a carport. Like our own house, they located theirs among rundown older adobe homes. We considered ourselves middle class, yet the differences with our neighbors were stark. Despite these differences, my parents were generous and friendly with all our neighbors. But the friendship took place at a distance for I saw none of those neighbors invited to our house. Instead, I only saw the same folks making up my parents' tight social circle.

Meals and school work at the new house created vivid memories of childhood primarily because they provided a sense of reassurance given how structured they were. The constancy tickled my sensitivity to order. Breakfast happened at 7:00 a.m., lunch at noon, and dinner at 6:00 p.m. on a regular clock-like basis. Dad never missed a meal, as he always took a two-hour break from work around noon and left work at 5:30 p.m. The midday break meant the town closed for two hours, a tradition introduced by Spaniards. These early inhabitants came from a country where businesses closed their doors so the staff could take a long break and a short nap during the day's hottest hours. I remember my parents taking the requisite noon siesta, frolicking instead of sleeping, while the kids ran around rambunctiously. Such daily routines underscore a normal and happy childhood.

Other behaviors provided fodder to my overactive mind. An especially interesting routine involved how we arranged ourselves at specific positions around the table for meals. Dad sat at the head, with Mom to his left and Nora to his right. On Mom's left sat Jaimito. I sat on the other head position of the table, facing Dad, while Fatima sat to my left. I do not remember how these positions came to be, yet they speak of patriarchal and pecking order. Especially intriguing is how we instinctively knew our places.

Doing homework and studying also gave me an additional opportunity to observe this highly structured and ordinary world. School work typically began around 7 p.m. following dinner. The expectation to learn school lessons and recite them to our parents, usually Dad, triggered a slew of pleasing behaviors. For one, we competed for who would be first to practice, whether a history or math lesson. I found comfort in the endless repetition of the multiplication tables, as Dad and I paced back and forth in the living room. These lessons were soothing, powerful, and helpful. I learned those tables so well I now can perform simple math problems in my head quickly and without difficulty. Most of the time, the siblings competed for who would fall asleep first while studying—a common occurrence following a big meal. Even at a young age, I found all this social-learning behavior intriguing. The presence of such regularity and order produced a sense of comfort.

In retrospect, my life has been continuously engaged in understanding and confronting the causal nature of actions and events, including imagined ones. Before I discovered science, my worldview arose from and was influenced by religion and its sensitivity to magical thinking and magical realism. The assumption in that world is of an unknown that is much too scary to confront, with a Devil and devil-like creatures causing evil and havoc, creating the need for celestial beings who can save, protect, and guide us through this nightmare of a life. There is a strong presumption that all these beings, good and bad, exist in the real world. Festivals that celebrated the Day of the Dead or Day of the Devils made these presumptions come to life. I remember one such celebration when adults dressed up as the devil or little devils (diablitos), with fearsome masks, and would run around town scaring the heck out of children.

Easter and the Christmas holidays, from the beginning to the present day, also provided noteworthy examples of times when magical realism infused and transcended ordinary reality. The memories of these holidays were seared in my brain. Tradition (another word for order?) meant that for Christmas, Dad and I would go out to find and cut down the right pine tree for decoration. Every year he and I headed out to the woods close to home. We searched for the best-looking tree, which we brought home and placed in the same semi-large aluminum pail filled with rocks and sand. I don't remember the actual decorating, so attribute such activity to Mom and sisters.

We, especially the children, then waited for Santa's arrival, full of expectations of receiving all kinds of gifts. Santa or St. Nick, the enigmatic saint, distorted my perceptions and created an illusory and temporary happiness and never disappointed. The fairy-tale saint, angel, or being would bring the asked-for soccer ball, bows and arrows, guns, and other toys. The mystery of this being continued for six wonderful and innocent years.

Then, by random chance, when I was six, I stumbled on toys hidden in a closet before the appointed day. It didn't take me long to make the connection of Santa's existence and that Dad and Santa were the same. The discovery did not bother me much, as I assumed what I had always suspected, that Dad had powers beyond the normal. I replaced an unrealistic magical thought with a more realistic one. Thinking of this sort, while common in children, is less common in adults. Yet, I found suspending my beliefs critical to my well-being when, as an adult, I had to confront a growing crisis between my professional career and my personal beliefs.

E. Fateful Events

Dad's profession as a lawyer and judge required the family to move several times to different parts of the country, sometimes with less than positive or beneficial outcomes. Soon after my birth, the family found itself in the northern coastal area of the country, in a town called Tela, where we lived for three years. Tela is in the northern Caribbean coast of Honduras and where Fatima was born. Here the hot, humid, and uncomfortable climate made living unbearable as houses lacked central air-conditioning.

Nora in front of our house in Tela.

Fortunately, we lived near the beach where the sand and the water became a special, comforting place, especially for Mom, who learned to appreciate the openness and breezes of the ocean. I have hazy memories of wading into the water and playing with my siblings. These positive associations are likely the reasons why today I find inspiration and calmness while walking on the beach.

A sudden illness I contracted at around two years of age, which produced severe diarrhea and nearly caused my death, punctured the idyllic beach paradise. My parents would tell the story of how they agonized about my illness and could only resort to prayer. The lack of medicine and doctors in the neighborhood and the progression of the illness presaged that I might not survive. Dad would recall the constant pacing while holding me, as my crying continued nonstop. As the illness progressed and I got worse, they became helpless, hopeless, and began to make plans to bury their second child. A last-minute desperate attempt by a doctor trying a new medication brought about my recovery. For my parents, the miracle represented a rebirth and another chance for their child. For me, the event, when recalled, serves as a reminder of what death might have meant.

The possibility of having my life erased at such a young age makes me experience what Jimmy Stewart, the protagonist of the movie *It's a Wonderful Life*, experienced. When the angel offers Stewart the chance to see what life would have been like had he not lived, he recognizes the wonderment of life. Imagining my death and the total absence of experiences, and how it would have undone the tapestry of my life as I review it, is spine-chilling. This exercise helps me appreciate the gift life can be.

A few years after my near-death experience, two other fateful events transpired between my third and fourth year of life, making me aware of a growing individuality and the sense of a greater force watching over me. First, at age three, I became aware of when I began to think of myself as a separate, distinct individual. Until then, I had no awareness of a separate me—only of an undifferentiated consciousness. One day my sister, Nora, decided she did not want to play. In that very instant, my world shattered. I wanted to play, so how could she not? The awareness dawned on me, more a feeling than a conceptual understanding, that she and I were distinct, with different thoughts. I now recognize this individuation as a normal process all children go through. This is what psychologists call the development of a theory of mind: the ability we develop to distinguish self from others and to know others can think different thoughts. The unexpected and earth-shattering aware-feeling of becoming an individual, separate from others, produced sadness in my young mind—because it made me recognize a kind of aloneness.

Similar feelings of sadness followed another major event—the day Dad took me to work. He had likely taken me many times before, although this time is the only one I recall vividly. In my mind's eye, I see myself on the second floor kicking a soccer ball along a long marble-floor corridor while Dad works in an office down the hallway. Then, in a flash, I see the ball going over the small metal railing and without thinking me going after it. My next visual is waking up in a hospital bed with Nora screaming while looking at my puffed-up and distorted face. Dad would recall how he saw the ball, followed by me going over the railing. His first thought was that I would not survive the fall, as he rushed to pick up the crumpled body from the cement-covered yard on the first floor. I landed on my right side but miraculously did not suffer any broken bones or serious injury. According to my parents, this became my second miracle and second rebirth. The episode helped reinforce the magical thinking bubbling over into real life, that a heavenly, protective force appeared to be watching over me.

F. An Inquisitive Mind

For the next few years, my childhood was a series of normal, healthy, sad, and happy moments occasionally interrupted by significant shifts in aware-ness and transcendent moments feeding my curiosity and inquisitiveness. The persona of a studious student, good son, and soccer aficionado grew slowly. Then came a major event. I failed the final exam in kindergarten. The memory and shame of it remains frozen in my mind. I can picture the teacher, whose name I cannot recall, approaching and asking me a simple question. "Why do you want to go to first grade?" I don't recall crying, only freezing and not being able to answer the question. Wiser minds decided first grade could wait until I could answer this.

When I finally passed the test the following year, I began attending a private Catholic school, the Immaculate Conception (IC), and did so until the fourth grade. At IC, I blossomed as a student, thanks to the nuns who taught the classes. The nuns, secretive beings who reminded me of aliens since they looked alike with the same habit and head dressing, were actu-ally good teachers. In class, they played an engaging game. It began by the teacher asking questions concerning any academic topic. Whoever had the right answer got to move forward and replace the person in the next chair. Slowly and a chair at a time, the most knowledgeable student would end up occupying the coveted first chair in the first row. It was a version of Jeopardy for small children. The game awoke in me a desire to outdo and surpass my competitors and get to the first chair. I would study intensely every night to achieve such a goal.

Whether the nuns knowingly activated a pre-existing competitive drive in their students, or unwittingly cultivated the urge to compete through their teaching methods, is difficult to know. More likely, the inner drive resulted from the interaction between abilities already present and the spark these teachers provided in lighting the fuse. The outcome had unexpected and meaningful consequences for me, for it helped create a set of unconscious and semiconscious motivations and actions organizing my future academic mindset. The resulting brain reorganization jump-started the development of my inquisitive mind.

CHAPTER TWO
Finding a Spiritual Identity

I have no chains, restraints, nor handicap,
My life feels free when looking back.
But now, I know the truth of my condition,
For slowly, I have built a virtual prison.

A. A Questioning Nature

"Why did you paint the picture I needed to paint?" I quizzed my mother as she put the finishing touches on a picture of red and yellow flowers in a green vase. Our Grade Four teacher had been teaching art and had assigned us to paint, draw, or create a work of art to share with others the following week. When I got home and told Mom, she seemed more excited than me. I didn't realize she would take the assignment as her own project.

"This is what every parent does," she responded. "They make sure their baby doesn't make something ugly."

"But how do I learn to paint if I don't do it?" I responded, unsure of what she meant.

"Trust me," she replied with a smile, "you will learn."

My identity resulted from many factors, both internal and external. As a child, the most important external factors were my family, namely, parents and siblings. Mom's response to my school homework likely reflected her love but also her own insecurities in her willingness to help me so much. And by doing so she created in me a particular set of expectations regarding parental roles, i.e., the need to be perfect, to pretend, to portray a certain social status, to depend on her, the need to avoid failure, and an unfounded optimism that things would turn out all right. What drove Mom's behavior? I do not know, but in looking back, I assume there was a level of maternal care and support, as well as pride, involved. It is also clear she worried about her social standing and that anything I did would reflect badly on her. She seemed to need a certain social appearance in the eyes of her peers, which might have been a stronger drive than the one to allow her own child to learn, make mistakes, and become an individual agent. Or, it could have simply been nurturing, feminine behavior.

Ever since my formative years, I have asked questions regarding why behavior and circumstances are as they are. This strong internal force became a foil to the external forces trying to impose a certain character or personality on me. In my mind, inquisitiveness shaped my identity the most, for it led me through the thicket of life experiences to find and focus on those things more meaningful to me. It helped me to find an identity. Like Mom's response, my questions were rarely answered to my satisfaction. They hid meanings my young mind could not comprehend but which struck me as not right and led to more questions. Eventually, I came to recognize this inquisitiveness as both a gift and a curse. The gift part propelled me toward science and down the road of exploring what I now consider the greatest mystery of all—the relationship between the human brain and the mind. It made me into a scientist. The approach science takes to get at truth involves its relentless questioning, in a structured way, with hypothesis drawn and tested until it leaves nothing but the simplest account that can logically explain it. The scientific approach matched, to a small degree, what I sensed in my questioning, and when the two came together the combination resembled finding my way home—it felt right!

B. Pleasure in Reading

My inquisitiveness also made me a voracious reader, for where else could I find the answers to my many questions? Books were a logical place. Finding answers provided an initial motivation for reading. Until I found that reading itself brought a kind of pleasure unlike what I experienced in other parts of living. The pleasure ignited an imagination that produced more pleasure by its simple exercise. If I did not eat or play, I read. I remember this reading pleasure as a strong physical reaction in which a warm feeling would flow from the top of my head down into the rest of my body. I literally would close my eyes to experience this wonderful warmth slowly seeping into every pore of my body, which I associated with the new and fascinating insights the book provided.

When young, my passion focused on comic books and the fantastic world they described—Batman, Superman, Spider Man, and my favorite, the Flash. I collected and read dozens of these. I would then trade the ones I finished for others my friends had. The supply proved inexhaustible, as all my friends had comic books which cost five to ten cents to buy. I identified with these comic heroes, their enemies were my enemies. I mimicked them and wanted to be like them. The lessons in morality were not overt, yet as Batman defended the poor and frightened citizens of Gotham, the lessons became as real as those heard at church.

Looking back, I now realize other types of books, what I would characterize as adult comic books, began to draw my attention away from children's comics. These were books on the drama of the human condition or human psychology. These books, although inevitably generating more questions and the need to read more books, answered my hunger for understanding the whys of human behavior. Why are habits so hard to change? Why do we treat others so badly? Why do we have such a hard time understanding others? Not every book produced the pleasurable, warm feeling, but those that did, I paid attention to.

As a teenager, my half-hearted relationship with religion began to change, and I began searching for books touching on those mysteries. Nothing seemed more remote and unreachable than divine and ultimate explanations. Yet, gradually this "unknown" began to have a strong pull on my attention, and my physical reaction to these books grew stronger. These are the books that have been attracting me since that time. My concept of the ultimate and ultimate concerns has evolved, however, from what I learned in Catholic catechism. Instead of a distant, unexplained, and unknowable presence, I now sense its source in my awareness, in my breathing, and in the warm physical reaction I get when reading.

C. The Downside of Inquisitiveness

While a questioning mind can be a gift, the behavior also carried a downside, particularly with regard to religion. Raised as a Roman Catholic, my questioning highlighted the clear boundaries existing around certain topics. In those days, Catholics, including children, made their Confession to a priest before taking Holy Communion. The priest would sit inside a confessional, literally a small armoire or portable closet with three small chambers. The priest occupied the middle one while sitting on a chair. On either side were the other chambers in which the faithful would kneel while speaking to the priest. Time after time, I remember entering the confessional with nothing to say. As a child, I could not remember committing any sins. Yet, I felt compelled to exaggerate and even lie just to say, I had confessed my sins. To my young mind, the exercise seemed irrelevant and wrong.

I recall asking my parents, "Why do I have to go to Confession when I have nothing to say?"

Invariably my Mom would look at me quizzically and remind me of the fight I had with my sister Nora. "It's my toy and I shouldn't have to give it to her," I would reply.

Tried as she could, Mom could not make me see the sin in not sharing toys. "I still think that's not what Father Joaquin wants to hear," I continued. "Doesn't he want to know who I killed or what I stole from the store?"

The crystal-clear logic made sense to me, for these were real sins, not pretend ones. Thus, the necessity of going through the charade of confession seemed a waste of time. My parents' response, after giving up on trying to argue with my logic, fell on the old conundrum that teachings required blind faith. I did not like those answers, for they implied I lacked control over most of my actions and other people or things had a greater say in determining whether my actions were right or wrong. I slowly began to withdraw from these teachings of the church and began looking elsewhere for better answers. This slow separation from Catholic dogma affected my first Communion, an especially important rite of passage and an exciting event for those undergoing it. I don't remember it and not sure I had one, a feeling I attribute to my decreasing interest in the religion. What I remember is not seeming to care.

D. A More Enlightened Experience

My search for a more enlightened experience took many years to find fruit. I found it is possible to find the right balance: to have an inquiring mind, to probe into life's mysteries, even the mystery of God, and to not experience guilt but a strengthening instead. I found questioning makes possible a deeper understanding of such mysteries and, in fact, a sense of acceptance when the mysteries seem impenetrable. I found this more open and healthier attitude in my exploration of science and then Buddhism, in particular Zen Buddhism, and more recently in the ideas of Advaita Vedanta or nondualistic thinking.

To my surprise, I have recently discovered a similar mindset in Christianity. However, such a treasure exists in only the books of mystics and saints, which few Christians know and read. I find it in books such as *The Cloud of Unknowing* and *The Book of Privy Counseling* by a fourteenth-century unknown Englishman and mystic, and *The Dark Night of the Soul* by St. John of the Cross. The arguments made by these mystics is contrary to those of science where materialism is primary. Instead, spirit is the transcendental and important aspect of life. This spirit lies beyond language and intellectual understanding, which, as the Buddhists argue, are fingers pointing to the moon and not the moon itself. By that I mean that the labels we use and the thinking we experience are not the actual spirit we seek. The mystics emphasize that all humans possess a faculty to know such a spiritual presence directly, yet rarely exercise it.

What is this faculty? It is the capacity for grace and love. This, however, is not the love we think of, such as Agape or Eros, for true love is a force that *destroys* the ego, the pretenses, the self-deception, and the falsity of being. This love and grace, and not concepts, grasp God, as William Johnston has written so beautifully. These mystical writings amazed me, for the mindset expressed in them resonated with my developing mindset and understanding. It's a mindset existing in the lives of the many who have sought spiritual truth, not just mystics, saints, Buddha, and Christ himself. Unfortunately, such openness to questioning and understanding is de-emphasized and a little-known and little-spoken aspect of Christianity.

Finding a spiritual identity does not happen overnight. It is an ongoing process. Fortunately, a strong inner inquisitiveness shone a light into this unknown, attracting me to specific ideas and emotions matching my inner feelings, and guiding the process. Along the way, this has allowed me to discard unimportant things not relevant to my development.

CHAPTER THREE
Beginning a New Life

I fell into the deep abyss of sleep.
And heard the high, continuous, piercing hum
That spoke to me in measured tones,
And said, "Wake up!"
And brought me back to life.

A. Letting Go of Everything

Opportunities in Honduras in the 1960s, not unlike today, limited anyone wishing to express their talents and live a good life. Thus, going abroad appeared as a reasonable option. To give us a better future, my parents made that ultimate sacrifice. They decided to send a child of theirs to study abroad. Such an option favored those who could afford such an alternative or whose circumstances made such a plan workable. We were lucky in having family members already living in Los Angeles, California. That fact determined the destination.

Since childhood and mainly because of the movies I watched, I imagined the United States as the land of plenty and of infinite possibilities. My parents' plan required whoever went to finish grade school, complete high school, and then return home. A U.S. high-school education would guarantee a successful life in Honduras. For one, that person would learn English, which would open up possibilities of attending English-only schools at home and the likelihood of a good job.

For my parents, their first and obvious choice centered on Nora, the eldest child. As they would tell us, they grew increasingly reluctant to send a lone female on such an unpredictable adventure. Honduras remains a patriarchal society where men see their role as protecting women from the harshness and realities of life. Reluctantly, my parents turned to their second-born male child. My gender provided my lucky break, and it would not be the last time.

In January 1963, as a nine-year-old, I went to live in a suburb of Los Angeles called Hawthorne. This new big bang in my life occasioned the beginning of an entirely new way of life. To make it possible, I had to detach from my immediate family, my friends, the environment I knew and loved so well, my culture, my native language. I had to let go of everything defining me.

For anyone, letting go is quite difficult, especially when it's a volitional choice, less so when it's imposed. To let go of your child in hopes they will have opportunities for a better future is a monumental sacrifice for parents to make. Ignorant of the huge burden it bore on them, I have often wondered whether I would have the same courage to send a child of mine thousands of miles away seeking an uncertain future. I can imagine the psychological trauma, guilt, and burden it would have on the parent and child. Yet, I often ask, why did this not leave me traumatized? Why do I not have any long-term scarring or regrets from being removed from my family and environment at such a young age? Why have I rarely focused on the negative aspects of this sacrifice? Why was letting go easy for me?

A partial answer to these questions is that I was young and adaptable. I also considered that I might be fooling myself and that it was indeed traumatic. I am an optimist by nature, one who looks at the positive side of things. And I forget the negative more easily than the positive. It's a mind with which I was born. Or, perhaps it was easier to adapt when the letting go was beyond my control, as it happened to the nine-year-old me.

Regardless, I see my parents' sacrifice as an immense and incalculable gift they gave me.

Uncle Joe and his family

B. Preparing for a New Life

My Uncle Joe, as I learned to call him, lived in Hawthorne, California, a suburb of Los Angeles, with his wife and three children, and became my personal liberator. Along with his wife, Cora, and their three young daughters, Rose, Livia, and Joyce, and paternal grandmother Livia, they agreed to take and raise me for a time. Uncle Joe and his family flew to Honduras in the early 1960s to arrange for my stay with them. During their visit, Joyce, the three-year-old and youngest daughter, requested a new and exotic food. She wanted French fries and became hysterical, as a three-year-old is wont to do when told there were no French fries in town, or likely the entire country, for there were no McDonalds or Burger Kings in Honduras at that time. Uncle Joe spent a few seconds explaining Joyce's object of desire. When he finished, I realized I also wanted French fries. "Quiero papas fritas," I uttered. My request seemed as good as saying I wanted to go to the United States

Uncle Joe and his family became my ticket to a better life. To prepare for the trip, I began saying good-bye to my friends. I knew I would never see them again. I vividly recall riding in the car a few weeks before my departure, with Dad driving and Mom in the front passenger seat. As we turned down a street, I saw my friend Pablo walking in his slow-moving way of his. I opened the car window, stuck my head out and shouted, "Adios Pablo–para siempre" meaning "Goodbye Pablo–forever." The cry-prediction of the child came true and I would not see Pablo ever again. Even now, the thought of losing such a friendship saddens me.

As part of the preparations, Dad and I visited the American Embassy in Tegucigalpa, the capital, to get a passport and visa. The two-hour drive from home seemed endless. I had recently turned nine and was excited regarding the prospect of flying, wishing the adventure would begin immediately. My young mind could not countenance delays. Likely there were issues trying to get the passport or visa, for I recall walking out of the embassy holding Dad's hand and seeing his worried look. In a serious voice, I said, "Dad, what will I do if I have to stay here?" I seemed to have decided that there was no other option other than going abroad. Dad, in his wise way looked at me with his sad countenance and responded, "When you are in Los Estados Unidos, study anything but law." The sudden focus on my education meant my trip would happen, although his comment regarding not studying law in the States spoke volumes regarding his assessment of the professional career he had pursued. His angst surprised me.

My impending trip intensified everyone's feelings and prompted wonderful expressions of caring. During the same trip to the capital to get the passport and visa, Dad bought a going-away gift that spoke volumes regarding his love for me and his concern for my religious upbringing. We had gone shopping in the downtown area of Tegucigalpa. I soon noticed all the stores we entered were jewelry stores. He must be trying to find a present for Mom, I thought. At the fourth store, he became more talkative and smiled, pleased in having found the right jewelry for her. The clerk wrapped it up, Dad paid, and we left. Half an hour into our trip back home, he leaned over to the glove compartment, took out the wrapped box and handed it to me.

"I want to give you this so you can remember me when you are in the States," he said.

I looked puzzled, for I still thought the gift belonged to Mom. Besides, no one had ever given me jewelry. The gift must be a watch, I thought, as I opened the box. Instead, a shiny gold necklace with a small crucifix attached against a heart-shaped background fell out. It was beautiful and I did not know what to say as I put the necklace around my neck.

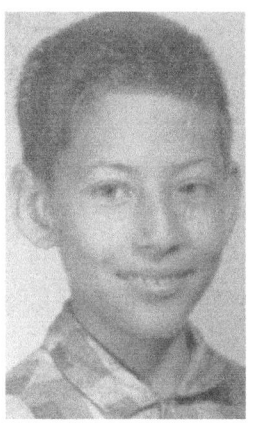

Dad's gift of the Christ necklace   *Me at nine years of age*

"I want you to wear Christ next to your heart all the time," Dad continued, referring to the necklace in a personal and religious way.

The hopefulness of his gift, as a counterpoint to the angst he had expressed earlier, combined the magical thinking and realism pervading my life. I use the term magical thinking in retrospect because at the time I did not know of life's connectedness and of the power and meaning of faith.

As luck would have it, Dad's present wasn't the only special going-away gift I received. Mom also gave me a rather special one. In her case, she chose the small Catholic missal she used. The small book had been her special and personal daily guide to prayer. On the second page of the missal, Mom, in her neat handwriting wrote, "Son: when you open this missal, may your thoughts rise up to God and pray for your parents and siblings who love you so much. Your Mom, Marietta." The fact both of my parents' gifts were religious spoke volumes regarding the supernatural protection they so readily sought and likely prayed for as I embarked on an uncertain future. I wore the Christ for many years until as a young adult I could no longer do so because of my changing views on religion. But I still keep and treasure both presents, for they ultimately represent the essence of the love my parents felt for me.

C. Leaving the Old, Finding the New

In 1963 at nine years of age, I left home for a promised Heaven. I did not realize how difficult the decision to let me go would be for Mom. Although she eventually agreed, she felt the decision had been forced on her. In her anguish, she wrote despondent letters to Aunt Cora, accusing her of stealing her baby. The meanness of the letters reflected a mother's pain. These letters created many awkward moments and produced long-lasting hurt feelings in both families.

Removing me from Mom's protective hug also produced sadness and anxieties in me. Dad designated himself as the one to pry me away, forcefully so I could board the plane. These scenes happened multiple times over the years, especially after visiting during the summer months and needing to return in September for the start of school. Mom would bearhug me and not want to let go. "Mi hijo," she would sob and then go limp when Dad tried to separate us. These emotional goodbyes created painful snapshot memories of a searing quality still lingering in my mind.

I flew alone on Pan Am airlines to Los Angeles the first time. Friendly stewardesses made sure I made the connections and felt comfortable. Aside from the emotional separation, the most memorable experience from the trip was seeing Los Angeles at night. An endless blanket of twinkling lights greeted me, covering the entire terrain my eyes could see from the small window. Not having flown before or been to a large city, I had never seen so many lights. I thought I had literally arrived in Heaven.

My first few days in LA were novel and exciting. I met many new people and discovered new surroundings. But soon I would encounter the one person who would mold me into her ideal version of a young man. The reality that I would not see my parents and siblings for a long time dawned on me soon thereafter and the sadness of those thoughts rolled in like an afternoon thunderstorm, bringing tears I could not willingly stop for several days. At that moment, I felt small, alone, and unloved.

Grandma Livia

Grandma Livia, my paternal grandmother, became my actual caretaker and I would live with her for the next eight years. She had been born in another century, in 1884, and now in her seventies, her child-rearing days were long behind her. She lived alone in an apartment apart from the main house where my uncle's family lived. Grandma Livia followed a traditional Christian lifestyle. The rosary, prayer, and saints were her constant companions and the chanting-like sounds of her prayers filled the apartment continuously. Grandma Livia looked at me as her ultimate project. As a former educator, of serious demeanor and strict, she brought to bear all the techniques and disciplines she had developed when teaching others. For a long time, I thought she could not smile.

Her first lesson which began right away involved teaching me daily prayers, an activity my parents had neglected to instill in me. Each night I would kneel next to my bed and repeat the prayers, while Grandma stood at the doorway like a guardian angel. Soon enough I learned the prayers by heart. The nightly ritual became routine, and my questioning began. Initially, the prayers had meaning but repetition dulled such meaning and literally put me somewhere else when I would say them. Why do I have to say the same prayer every night? Is God that forgetful that I have to repeat the same thing every day? Why doesn't He answer them? Are prayers not spoken from the heart received? Grandma Livia didn't have time for such questions. They added to my growing discontent with religion.

Her unrelenting discipline gained more prominence and became the dominant struggle between us. She initially demanded I not watch TV until I completed my homework. Her initial request seemed like a reasonable sacrifice until the rule morphed into no TV at all during the week, only on weekends. I went along kicking and screaming. I could watch morning cartoons on weekends, which I enjoyed. Then, the television had to be off until 7:00 p.m. on Saturdays and then we would only watch shows she wanted to watch like *The Lawrence Welk Show* or *The Ed Sullivan Show*. My young mind rebelled, for I knew there were more exciting action shows to watch like *Star Trek* and *Gunsmoke*, yet I could never win an argument with Grandma Livia. Like an old Michelangelo persistently chipping away at her block of granite, she slowly sculpted me into an even more studious student, or at least her view of what a studious person is. I deeply resented her efforts–in fact, I hated her.

For a long time, I did not appreciate the discipline she instilled in me, the ability to overcome my desires for momentary things and postpone gratification. Her discipline represented her way, I reasoned, of showing me her love. My resentment then became a deep appreciation. The most positive and endearing memory of living with Grandma Livia is the vision of her chasing me around the apartment with a long wooden spoon to get me into the shower. Left to my own devices, I would only shower once a week.

She also made oatmeal with canned peaches and scrambled eggs with a shredded tortilla for breakfast. Her relentlessness taught me good personal hygiene. I disliked the oatmeal and peaches, but thought the egg dish with shredded tortilla as the most delicious of meals. I rarely eat oatmeal now and if I do, I want peaches in it. Scrambled eggs with a shredded tortilla are a must and what I share with everyone for whom I cook breakfast.

Shortly after my high-school graduation in June, 1971, Grandma Livia passed away. She had acquired dementia by then and could no longer recognize anyone, including me, Dad, or Uncle Joe. An era had ended, not in a way most had expected yet naturally. They buried her in the hills of LA at the Holy Cross Cemetery in Culver City, California. When I drive through LA now, I sense her gaze directed toward me from above and it reminds me of evening prayers, oatmeal, and shredded tortillas. Grandma Livia lives on in me.

Uncle Joe, who was Grandma Livia's second child, had been a true free spirit. During the Second World War, he joined the U.S. Merchant Marine, got U.S. citizenship and settled in California with his family in search of a safer and better life. His dream of attending school and studying mechanical engineering, unfortunately, did not materialize for a variety of reasons. Instead, Uncle Joe trained to become an airline mechanic and ended up working for Trans World Airlines (TWA), a large and well-known domestic and international airline existing from 1930 to 2001. At one time, the billionaire Howard Hughes, an engineer, owned TWA and my uncle deeply respected him.

Through initiative and hard work, Uncle Joe became the chief supervisor of a group of mechanics whose main task ensured planes could fly safely. As much as he achieved in life, Uncle Joe never overcame a sense of disappointment and unhappiness. I think he saw in me the potential materialization of his own dreams. Toward the end of his life, his unhappiness resolved into an ennui, catapulting him to take up drinking, and to suffering a stroke.

Soon enough, his drinking problem spread to his relationship with his children, especially the oldest, Rosemarie or Rose, as we call her. Rose resembled her dad in having an indomitable and unquashable free spirit. The tension between the two increased and became more palpable as his drinking worsened and she grew up into young adulthood. Inevitably, the tension produced moments of conflict and shouting through the apartment I lived in. I remember one particular Saturday morning waking up to what sounded like muffled shouting and banging sounds coming from outside. I scurried to the small kitchen window overlooking the main house but could not see anything, except the screaming got louder and more distinct.

"Didn't I tell you to be home by 11 p.m. last night," I heard Uncle Joe say in an angry voice. "Why are you sneaking into the house at 3 a.m.? What do you think this is? This is not your home, this is my home and I make the rules," he continued in his angry and loud voice.

I heard Rose's voice faintly through the sobs. "I'm sorry, Dan and I were out and lost track of time. We did nothing wrong."

I could localize the sounds coming from the laundry room in the back of the main house, off to my left. After fifteen minutes the door opened and Rose ran out crying back to the main house, followed by Uncle Joe, with a belt in his hands. Given my quietness, patience, and nonrebellious character, I had a different relationship with Uncle Joe. During his hours-long monologues with me, which he took as moments to advise, he continually praised and encouraged me. As I sat there stoically, he would repeat in his slightly inebriated state "Jaime, you are the family jewel. Keep studying and do well in school." It made me happier and grateful I did not provoke him to anger.

D. A Growing Self-Consciousness

The studiousness and discipline Grandma Livia instilled in me helped with the challenges of school, academically and otherwise, at a time of growing self-consciousness. Soon after my arrival in the States, I began school life at Hawthorne Elementary School. Only a few blocks from home, I began by repeating the fourth grade, which I had completed in Honduras. My teacher, Mrs. Alba, spoke Spanish and made me welcome. Her first question to me was whether I preferred Jaime (the Spanish pronunciation) or Jamie (the Anglicized one). The question took me by surprise. I responded I preferred to use my real name (the Spanish one), unaware my agreement with Mrs. Alba made little difference to everyone else who preferred to call me Jamie. Over time, my preference for the Anglicized sound grew to the point the Spanish pronunciation of Jaime began sounding foreign and strange.

How I signed my name reflected my changing personality. Until then, my signature resembled Dad's, which I had purposely copied. His moniker must have reflected unconscious desires for stature since the ornateness of the signature was grandiose. It was not right for me. I simplified it to reflect my own developing character by settling on printing the J and P of my first and last names in a slanted manuscript style. Simplifying my signature reflected a growing self-consciousness. Despite the many challenges resulting from adjustments to a new culture and ongoing changes in my personality, I transitioned through grade school successfully. I skipped Mrs. Waller's fifth-grade class, which made up for my lackluster performance in kindergarten. I also did well in Mrs. Santos' sixth-grade class.

Throughout this time, my secret weapon in doing well in these classes turned out to be a complete Encyclopedia Britannica at my uncle's house. The encyclopedia proved to be an invaluable resource and a lifesaver. Uncle Joe, or maybe Aunt Cora, had purchased the thirty-two-volume set at a high cost, reasoning the resource would help their daughters academically. As fate would have it, no one benefitted more than I did once I discovered it.

During sixth grade, Uncle Joe took me to work one day. We headed to LA International or LAX as most people knew it. I remember the TWA facilities and climbing into a large plane and exploring the inside while

Uncle Joe gave out instructions to the other mechanics. He then took me outside to see the jet engines. Their size awed me, as they could easily hold my four feet eight inches frame standing up. Uncle Joe's explanation of the concept of how a jet engine takes air and causes lift fascinated me. I left thoroughly impressed by the environment he worked in and most especially by him as a knowledgeable and smart person. It wasn't too long after that I did a science poster on jet engines and how they make flying possible. The poster reflected all Uncle Joe had told me on the visit, plus what I learned from the encyclopedia. The report received a science award for its detailed nature and graphical presentations.

I credited many fine reports and presentations to the encyclopedia and Uncle Joe. To hear that the last printed edition of the encyclopedia would be published in 2010 caused me deep sorrow. I continued using it in middle school where I also did well and enjoyed the lessons of Mrs. Calhoun in the seventh grade and Mrs. McClung in the eighth grade. My intellectual identity had developed well despite the radical change in culture and language.

E. The Dark Side of Growing Up

Around the beginning of eighth grade, a new and unexpected set of incidents happened. A darker side of life showed itself as I became the recipient of bullying behavior. Why this started then and not before is unclear, but I suppose I can blame it on teenagehood, or as the Urban Dictionary describes it, "when everyone in school starts giving you looks and whispering giddily for other reasons than you just walked out of the bathroom with toilet paper on your shoe." I recall walking out of the school grounds at Hawthorne Elementary School and heading home when I saw Don and two other eighth-grade classmates hanging out by the stop sign. Don towered over most other eighth graders, but I thought nothing of it until I felt his push from behind.

"What are you doing?" I shouted as I turned and faced my classmates.

"Teacher's pet," came the reply in a pretend-meanness loudness. "Why don't you go back where you came from," he continued. "You're black or Mexican, aren't you?" Don piped in as he followed me. "What's someone like you doing in our neighborhood?" he asked derogatorily to no one in particular.

They used words I did not understand as I kept walking trying to get away from him and the others. They followed me and after several pushes from behind, took off running. This would happen a couple more times. For me, the names they accused me of, such as "teacher's pet" or "brain," didn't produce the expected response since they seemed more like compliments. However, other names were more hurtful. As much as I did not like the pushing and the taunting, the ignorance they displayed regarding Honduras bothered me as well. Inexplicably, the Central American bridge had disappeared during geography class or at the least they seemed to feign ignorance rather well.

Recalling this episode of bullying in eighth grade makes me realize that I have not experienced such overt behavior since. Vulnerability at that point in my life made sense having undergone significant changes in circumstances. It was this vulnerability, I am convinced, that allowed the bullying experience to occur. Such an experience continued the fortification of the psychological protective shell guarding my fragile sense of self. Once I found my grounding, I did not project as much vulnerability. Also, because these episodes were short-lived and mild, they do not seem to have affected or traumatized me in significant ways. Nonetheless, all such events have a role in defining and guiding us in a certain direction. The incidents made me aware of a dark side of growing up that temporarily colored my perspective, expectations, and sense of self during the beginning of high school.

CHAPTER FOUR
Developing an Intellectual Identity

I sit waiting at the open door.
Waiting patiently for the signal,
For there must be a signal
To enter such an important place.

A. Growing Psychological Challenges

As a child, my personality projected quietness and confidence, but this confidence began to erode quickly amid my new environment and the seismic changes in the new circumstances. For one, I had become an outsider scorned and laughed at. I no longer commanded respect from friends and classmates. My peers did not see me as a leader. Coupled with the inevitable hormonal changes flooding my adolescent mind, my quietness gained a tinge of low self-esteem and fearfulness. I became painfully shy and insecure by the time I entered high school. With little confidence in what I knew and did not know, my inner sense of worth disappeared completely. I began judging myself relative to others, with a sense of lack and becoming increasingly self-critical. An inner critic bloomed. This intensification of my self-consciousness highlighted thoughts regarding my personality and sense of self. My mind became sensitive of its own existence. Part of this increased self-consciousness involved the loss of trust in the reality around me and a sense of the loss of control I thought I had.

High school became a time to grapple with this growing set of challenges threatening my self-identity. Hawthorne High School (HHS), which

I attended from 1967 to 1971, required a twenty-five-minute walk, which gave me time to engage in unending self-analysis and discussion regarding my psychological trials. I disposed of a few problems, yet others overwhelmed me. I never felt I could bring these difficulties home to Grandma Livia or Uncle Joe, let alone anyone else. I felt very alone.

I engaged in prolonged internal dialogue with myself throughout the four years of high school. The lack of adult guidance permitted several regrets to form, and participation in sports headed the list. As a soccer enthusiast, I badly wanted to join the high-school soccer team, yet my shyness and fear of the new culture prevented me from trying out. I could have used advice from a fatherly figure, but unfortunately Uncle Joe had his own family issues and did not have time to focus on me. In fact, Uncle Joe took me to a ball field only once to play catch, so we never bonded in that respect.

An even bigger regret involved girls and dating. Figuring out girls and this rather unique and complicated American ritual was my responsibility. Although females drew my interest and one or two classmates appeared interested in me, I could not overcome my reluctance to ask anyone out. I blame this reluctance and growing shyness for the fact I did not attend senior prom and in the process missed out on the Beach Boys who, at the height of their fame, were the headliners. Apparently, several members of the band had attended HHS. Missing out on such a unique celebration became a significant regret.

Overall, these are the memories I keep under a psychological rug. When they get exposed, the feelings of remorse, guilt, and disappointment can be strong.

B. Encountering the World of Literature

More positive aspects of growing up balanced teenage angst and psychological issues. For one, I remember high school for the many new ideas it exposed me to. High on the list was the introduction to great literature and poetry. Teachers at HHS fostered my desire to know the classics and fed my voracious reading appetite. Thus, I read Hawthorne, Cooper, Steinbeck, Hemingway, and European authors such as Hugo, Dickens, Tolstoy, and others. These classics were all I wanted to read, as if in a race to catch up. To me these works represented the distilled experience of humanity. They engaged my imagination, for they spoke in a universal language exposing both the foibles and nobility of the human condition. I didn't know this made them classic novels—I just enjoyed them.

Unconsciously the stories reinforced specific Western cultural norms and behaviors I took as my own. I remember reading the *Grapes of Wrath* by John Steinbeck and wanting to have the grit and fortitude of the Joad clan as they journeyed from Oklahoma to California only to find disappointment in the paradise they expected. I eventually realized what a biased view of life I had gained from these books, which did not include perspectives from my own Latin culture or from other typically ignored literatures, such as African literature.

Once exhausted with the classic genre, I discovered science fiction. I read Asimov, Bradbury, Orwell, and other Nebula Award winners. Asimov and his books on robots were my particular favorite. In this genre, I saw the future, or at least the potentialities of what humanity could become, good or bad. Although even dystopian-like stories such as George Orwell's *1984* seemed hopeful in their warnings to the reader. The stories provided what I needed to exercise my active imagination.

C. Language of Poetry

High school also inspired my deep interest in poetry. I can pinpoint the exact moment when this interest expressed itself. During the ninth-grade English class, the teacher had assigned us to write a poem in any style. Until then, poetry for me equaled rhythm and rhyme. Hard as I tried, I could not make two sentences rhyme. Then, Andy McCain read his poem and what I heard floored me. The reading of his poem set off a small explosion in my brain.

Andy would become the salutatorian of the class after Rick Mercurio, our valedictorian. Andy's poem did not rhyme and appeared more conversational and stream-of-consciousness, yet the teacher thought his work deserved an award for best effort. As the teacher explained, Andy had written in free verse, which has no set meter, no rhyme scheme or any structure, yet gives the writer license to be creative without rules. From this small mind explosion grew my desire to write poetry in free verse and to read poets who wrote this way.

Since then I have read many poets. Two of whom I most admire and have tried to emulate over the years are Walt Whitman and Emily Dickinson, considered the father and mother, respectively, of free-verse English poetry. They are also two of America's most important poets and continue to inspire me.

My crude attempts at free verse began in high school. Initially my poems had a stream-of-consciousness quality to them. I struggled to direct this motivating drive into a coherent force. But a mind without the correct insight partially obscured the ideas. Only until my early forties, when life began to make more sense, did the stream-of-consciousness effort began to change to a conscious effort with a thoughtful reflection of themes.

D. Practical Pursuits

High school represented the beginning of several intellectual and practical pursuits which continue to reverberate in my life. None was more important and practical in terms of outcomes than the opportunity offered to senior students at the local Regional Occupational Center. It had recently begun offering courses for those interested in learning a potentially good trade, including computer programming. I don't recall why programming classes appealed to me, as I knew nothing regarding computers and the languages used to run them. Yet they attracted me. Perhaps because of the possibility that they would facilitate employment as a programmer. Not many of my classmates took up the offer.

The whole episode reminded me of a similar experience two summers before when a typing class had likewise attracted me. I had been the only male in the class of twenty students. The experience made me uncomfortable, yet I learned to type on an old IBM Selectric typewriter. Why? Not sure what motivated me to enroll in that class, other than a strong sense that typing represented a skill I needed to learn. And Grandma Livia's insistence that I do something useful during the summer.

Now computer programming called. The punched cards we used, the sound they made as they read in the code punched into them, the bugs we had to correct, and eventually getting the right outcome fascinated and made me want to learn more. That year I learned to program in Common Business-Oriented Language (COBOL), a programming language for business data processing needs. COBOL is rarely used now, although it was popular then. The basics of programming learned with COBOL provided the stepping stool to learn FORTRAN, ASSEMBLER, BASIC and C++. More than anything, the experience made me comfortable with digital technology and unafraid to explore the inexhaustible offerings appearing every year.

Despite many challenges, I completed high school in 1971, graduating in the top 5% of thousands of students. I had begun high school shy and lacking in self-confidence, yet by the end, I had gained more confidence. I had read more and became fascinated by the exploration of digital technology. I exorcised the monsters faced in middle school, although perhaps not completely, namely, bullying behavior and feelings of self-doubt. There were still fearsome beasts lurking in my psychological closet, including anxiety, loneliness, and uncertainty of what the future would bring.

Encountering a Spiritual Mystery

Amid this uncertainty,
I hear the call unflinchingly.
Is it the product of a febrile mind?
One facing death?
Or, a true answer I need to find?

A. Protection

One afternoon in March 1970, I absent-mindedly was walking home from HHS feeling exhausted and with a head full of math calculations. I had not realized how engaging calculus was and had become obsessed with it. Calculus made sense, and I occasionally considered whether a career as a mathematician would interest me, even though I knew nothing of what they did. I remember a sunny yet cool day, typical of Southern California in winter. I didn't know I would soon experience another potentially ill-fated yet dreamlike event, helping to quiet my growing anxieties, loneliness, and uncertainty regarding the future.

Before crossing an intersection near the school, a shiny object on the ground caught my attention. Ever the curious one, I stopped and reached down to pick it up. I don't remember the object because at exactly that instant. I heard a loud screech from a car and saw it make a right turn at the intersection not stopping for the red light. Momentarily paralyzed, I likely dropped the object as the implications of what had happened dawned on me. Had I not stopped to pick up the shiny thing, an action taking only about five seconds, I might have entered the intersection and been run over. I would now be dead.

Deep in the recesses of my mind, I recognized with great gratitude the spiritual force that had spared me, for it seemed to reach out from the past but still surrounding and protecting me. A five-second distraction saved my life. The magical realism of my childhood made its presence known to the adolescent me. But this time it felt different, more concrete, more real. A feeling and knowing that life could be positive, and in fact that a vital and dynamic force could be on my side, strengthened my weakening confidence. Those thoughts lasted but a few seconds. It would be many years before these feelings would become more understandable.

B. Caring

Following high-school graduation in June 1971, I began attending classes at the University of California, Los Angeles (UCLA) in fall of 1972 while still living at home. No one, not my Uncle Joe, Grandma Livia, or parents, questioned whether I should plan a return trip to Honduras. I think my parents were justly proud and supportive I was starting university studies in the States They had conveniently forgotten the pact we had agreed to regarding returning home upon high-school graduation. I knew I had.

Attending university in the United States opened up a new world of possibilities. UCLA offered me a variety of scholarships and so made my decision to attend there easier. Arriving at the Westwood campus the first time, I felt small, alone, and uncertain. I had no friends and felt a million miles away from my birthplace. I don't recall Orientation Day other than being shuffled from one part of the campus to another. There were several things regarding the campus that stood out. For one, it was a huge space with an unusual number of green, grass-covered areas throughout, areas ringed by large pines, oaks, and other types of trees. Nestled in these forest-like oases were a combination of striking old architectural-style buildings. As I would learn, these were reminiscent of the twelfth-century

Lombard Romanesque style of southern Italy. The colors of the brick and limestone used, even for the more modern structures, represented the hot sun and bright light of the Mediterranean region. The campus struck me as a beautiful and a peaceful center for learning. I felt lucky to be there.

At noon during Orientation Day, they herded us into an eating area at Ackerman Union, the campus bookstore and center for socializing on campus. There seemed to be a large group of students taking part, so I grabbed the first open chair and began to partake of the lunch. As I did, the tallest person with the largest tennis shoes I had ever seen came in and sat down next to me. In a deep voice he introduced himself.

"I'm Bill, who are you?"

"I'm Jaime," I replied.

We chitchatted while we ate and I watched in marvel as Bill consumed plate after plate of the food available to us. I had not seen anyone eat so much before. I remember counting six empty plates piled on top of each other as we left. In the course of our conversation, I learned my friend Bill Walton, at six feet eleven inches, played basketball, which seemed to make sense. When I began to hear that the UCLA basketball team might win consecutive NCAA championships, it struck me that the Bill Walton I had met during orientation was the star of the basketball team. Bill made a name for himself in UCLA basketball history under Coach John Wooden, winning three consecutive College Player of the Year Awards and leading UCLA to two NCAA Championships in 1972 and 1973. I deeply regret not having asked Bill for his autograph while we sat and ate lunch together during freshman orientation. Unfortunately, I could not foresee the future.

I also learned that another famous cohort in the class had likely attended orientation—Jimmy Connors, the great tennis player. Connors won the NCAA singles title as a freshman in 1972 for UCLA and attained All-American status. I quickly realized I had entered a universe unlike any I had ever known.

My sense of loneliness and isolation, however, overwhelmed the seeing of new possibilities. And yet, moments of transcendence interrupted the gray constancy of my negativity. During enrollment in the fall, I stood in line to register for classes, anxious and hopeful the courses I wanted would still be available. A fellow behind me tapped me on the shoulder and asked me a question.

"What classes are you taking?" I heard him ask.

"I'm trying to get into the Math 101 and Chemistry 1A, and you?" I replied.

As we chatted, I noticed Rodolfo Boquin had a slight accent.

"Where are you from?" I asked.

What he said in reply took me by surprise, for I did not expect it.

"I'm a native of Honduras," he replied.

"Are you kidding me?" I almost snorted. "How can that be, I'm also from Honduras," I said.

He became equally surprised.

"I only know one other Honduran here at UCLA," he continued.

I didn't know anyone so his comment produced a cascade of thoughts regarding new potential friends. What we said next would produce a kind of dissociative experience I had never experienced before or since.

"Where in Honduras are you from," he asked nonchalantly.

"Comayagua," I responded.

Rodolfo's eyes got large, and it took several seconds before he clapped his hands and shouted, "No way, that's too weird. So am I."

His response surprised me for not only did he purport to be from Honduras, but now claimed to be from my specific hometown. The improbability shocked me and I felt numb for a few seconds. No one, I thought, except me has come from little, forgotten Comayagua to the

United States, especially to this world-class university. I had a hard time computing the probabilities.

"Who are your parents?" I asked incredulously.

After he told me his dad, also named Rodolfo Boquin, and known as Dr. Popo in town, I flashed to the clinic and the short-haired doctor I knew and remembered. Dr. Popo had been the only doctor in Comayagua for a long time. He was a family friend whom my parents consulted and knew socially. He undoubtedly had treated me for an illness or two. Because we lived on opposite sides of town, the son and I never knew each other well, yet here we were.

"When did you come to the States?" "Where do you live?" "Where is your family?"

We each had a thousand questions trying to understand what had just happened. There are coincidences and then there are miracles. This definitely felt like the latter kind. In the blink of an eye, I felt like a higher power had given me a gift and placed Rodolfo at the right time and place to ease what felt so overwhelming. The event temporarily eased my self-conscious chatter and my sense of separation and isolation. He and I talked for a long time and promised to get together in the near future. We said goodbye as we left. Unfortunately, I never saw Rodolfo again. Yet, the feeling of being watched and cared for by a providential and loving grace has stayed with me all my life.

C. Guidance

It wasn't long thereafter I sensed the same higher power again. I had started undergraduate life at UCLA as a math major since I had done well in the subject at HHS. But I quickly switched to Engineering, then Pre-medicine, and finally Sociology. I did not know what I wanted to study. The fact there were kids who were much smarter than I did not help my confidence. I struggled through freshman chemistry, barely earning a passing grade. In contrast, a friend who got an "A" told me he rarely studied because the material did not challenge him enough. I remember sitting side by side in class feeling disheartened and depressed.

Those feelings accompanied me to every class I took during the fall and winter quarters of the first year. In spring, I enrolled in Introduction to Psychology and things took a different turn. As the name suggests, the class introduced psychology to freshmen students who might want to pursue it as a major. The first day proved auspicious as I walked into the largest class I had ever attended. The semi-circular auditorium held about five hundred students, all talking at once. I settled down on a seat at the top of the auditorium, fortunate to have found one. As I sat there for five minutes waiting for the class to start, a young, short-haired male with glasses and sandals, who I assumed to be the professor, approached the podium. The loud noise settled down from a roar to a murmur and then complete silence as if a disk jockey had turned down the dial.

"Good morning," said the young academic to the silent crowd, "Welcome to Introduction to Psychology."

He then went over the syllabus and how students would be graded, the recommended textbook, where the various student sections would be held. After a few questions, the professor began his lecture, and it became immediately clear that I needed to pay attention.

Maybe it was the deep and mellow tenor of his voice, or his appearance as a tall and slim person, which caused me to lose track of everyone around me. Everyone literally disappeared as I became mesmerized by the professor's voice and his stories. The experience I recall played out with me as an observer hovering above the room. I saw myself as the lone figure listening to the teacher who stood at the bottom of the auditorium well. I had stopped thinking and just listened. I was totally fascinated by what we would learn in class throughout the quarter. And totally engaged by the examples the professor gave. On the history of psychology. Its founders in Europe and America. On current theories and issues in areas such as attention. Cognition. Motivation. And finally, on the importance of the scientific method and the principles of research design, which he would emphasize throughout the term.

At the end of the class and while the auditorium emptied, I felt disoriented. What had just happened? After a few seconds, I began to experience a warm feeling and a sense I had stumbled upon what had been missing. It felt like I had found my way home after being lost, and a sense of relief, gratitude, excitement, and a budding awareness arose within now that I knew what I needed to do.

Halfway through the course, the professor assigned us to carry out an experiment outside of class. The exercise captured my interest and curiosity, namely, because of the ability to go out into the wild, collect data, and draw conclusions concerning an important question. It became a notable experience, especially because it involved working with a partner. I remember brainstorming with this lanky, glass-wearing male with short, wiry hair concerning what we could study. After contributing ideas, we finally settled on an approach, which I don't recall. What made an impact related to the way we gathered the data, namely, by having our subjects fill out a questionnaire. We then tallied the results and came up with our conclusions. I knew nothing of research until then, but felt an inner attraction. I found the assignment interesting.

After receiving an "A" in the class, I knew I would study psychology and declared it as my official and final major. The entire episode with Introduction to Psychology did not feel like a coincidence. I made a conscious choice to be there the first day, yet the choice itself felt beyond my control and inevitable. As I look back, I sensed the same mysterious force that had shadowed me throughout my life making itself more known, guiding me along a specific path, and making me more conscious of its presence. The experience definitely increased my confidence and slightly decreased my fear of the unknown.

D. Presence

Toward the end of my first year at UCLA, I drove home to Hawthorne one afternoon and encountered the same stealthy and mysterious force—this time in a more direct and unequivocal manner. I was cruising along above the speed limit in the fast lane on the 405 freeway. Barely aware of others around me, when suddenly a question zipped across my mind, "What would you do if the car in front of you stopped?" The thought differed from my regular thoughts, which were running at a thousand miles an hour. Above the din, I heard this question distinctly, and the answer came just as quickly—swerve onto the space to the left!

Immediately, the car in front of me slowed down considerably and I executed the plan and applied the brakes. I came to a stop, as did several other cars, but no one had hit anyone. A wave of relief and gratitude washed over me, for without this precognition, I would have likely plowed into the car in my lane. I knew "something" had gifted me another chance to avoid injury. Call it my spiritual protector or caretaker. Guidance counselor. A type of a direct heavenly instructor. Whatever it was, the mysterious force imbued with the magical realism of my childhood and adolescent years had made its presence known. I began to consider this force an intimate awareness, deeply caring power, providential, instead of the enigmatic, external, and mysterious force of previous years.

At this point in my life, I had retreated from my Catholic upbringing, rarely attending church, while only celebrating the major holidays like Easter and Christmas. The term is "lapsed Catholic." The rapping sound of a spiritual power at my doorstep kept getting louder, yet I still felt reluctant to acknowledge it. I had not yet started on any spiritual path but the one year at UCLA, where the described events occurred, were pointing me to things I needed to attend to.

PART II

DIGRESSIONS AND A CAREER

CHAPTER ONE
Military—High Price of Freedom

I choose the long way home.
Perhaps a deeply ingrained and
Unconscious desire to extend the journey.
To enjoy the slow and mindful drive.

A. Leaving My Second Home

Classes at UCLA were difficult but manageable. Family dynamics, on the other hand, were becoming unbearable and unmanageable. After Grandma Livia's death, I had moved in with Uncle Joe and his family in the main house. This was a three-bedroom California-style home with two apartments in the back, where Grandma Livia and I had previously lived. To make room for me, my cousins, Livia and Joyce, moved into the larger bedroom. I moved into the smaller one next to them. Rose, my oldest cousin, had married by this time and lived nearby. Aunt Cora and Uncle Joe had the master bedroom down the hallway.

The transition from living with my grandmother to living with the family proved difficult. My feelings of being enclosed and uncomfortable increased each day. I could sense the awkwardness of the presence of a male in a house full of females, except for Uncle Joe. I recall the first time I took a shower in the fuchsia-tiled bathroom I shared with my cousins. I can still hear the high-pitched scream Livia made when she walked in after I had finished. She found water all over the floor, and the shower doors dripping with water. Such chaos was unfamiliar to them. The stern reprimand from Aunt Cora, while appropriate, made me even more uncomfortable, "You will have to learn to be clean and to wipe down the shower stall, doors, and floor after you finish," she said. Her comment seemed to question Grandma Livia's training.

On the one hand, I knew I had to adjust and learn new rules. But, on the other, I didn't think I had done anything wrong. Why have tiles on the floor if not to get them slightly wet? Isn't a shower supposed to get the walls and doors wet? Why create so much work by having to dry it all down each time anyone showered? It made little sense to me. Although I complied, taking a shower from then on became an uncomfortable experience, for it took longer to clean the bathroom than to clean myself. It might have made more sense to me had Aunt Cora explained the reasoning behind the cleaning. Wet floors are a slip hazard. Not toweling off wet surfaces promotes mildew growth and mineral residue accumulation on the tile and glass surfaces—which becomes increasingly difficult to remove in the long run. It might have helped!

I soon found out that explaining was not her style. Instead, she created unnecessary work like a master. She had never expressed, nor had I sensed, any inkling she liked me being part of the family. Perhaps she had soured on the plan my uncle had devised once my mother started her letter campaign accusing her of stealing me. Aunt Cora had little idea of what to do with a young boy growing into adulthood and so made up things for me to do. She routinely gave me a lot of work cleaning the yard, cutting the ivy plants covering the front lawn, washing all the windows in the house inside and out, and polishing brass furniture.

I quickly grew concerned she saw me as a servant ready to do anything and she needed to keep me busy all the time. The sense of entrapment and walking on eggshells so as not to disrupt the family environment made me want to leave without having to return to Honduras or become homeless. The search for freedom and independence without too much pain motivated me to seek alternatives.

At twenty years of age, the itch for independence had become unendurable. So, in 1973, after only one year at UCLA, I left the university and my second home to join the one organization providing an acceptable substitute: the U.S. military. I had briefly considered the Peace Corps and other such options, but the military provided the most attractive choice. After a bit of consideration concerning which service to join, I decided on the Air Force because of its reputation and promises of training. The pamphlets and other advertisements about the Air Force made it seem more professional than the other services.

Uncle Joe felt disappointed and tried to dissuade me from dropping out of school and giving up on all the scholarships I had. Aunt Cora likely had her cheering hat on for me to leave. As far as my decision to depart, I do not remember seeking permission from my parents or even asking for their advice. It broke the covenant we had agreed upon concerning my return once I completed my education in the States. But by now the sense of freedom, openness, and future possibilities overwhelmed any residual hankering I had to return to Honduras. When I visited my native land, I felt more like a stranger and could identify more with American tastes and culture. It felt too late to go back.

B. A New Sense of Freedom

Joining the U.S. Air Force proved simple and straightforward. I had to report for military duty on January in 1973. I don't recall saying goodbye to the family, although I must have, which shows how important leaving had become. I remember the flight from Los Angeles to San Antonio on a cool and sunny California day. A long bus ride from the San Antonio Airport to Lackland Air Force Base followed the flight. When we arrived, they herded us into a reception area holding hundreds of recruits, all of similar age, and given a brief welcome and introduction.

The following day, we lined up for the mandatory haircut and handing out of uniforms. I wondered how long cutting everyone's hair would take since there were so many of us. I didn't realize the haircut took under five seconds per recruit and literally a dozen stations made the line disappear rather quickly. Medical evaluations followed, with a quick checkup and vaccinations for what seemed dozens of diseases. To get the vaccinations, we walked in a single file between individuals in white coats on the left and right who gave us the vaccines using jet guns. After several painful shots, I lost count of how many more I received. What I do remember vividly was the high number of recruits fainting from the multiple injections. They were quickly dragged away to recover. The imagery is eerie as I reflect on it.

Boot camp at Lackland emphasized military discipline, how to march and how to shoot an M-16 rifle. To my amazement, I could march well enough and shoot accurately enough. This impressed the drill instructors, especially after I scored high in marksmanship. Mostly, however, the eight-week boot camp entailed screaming instructors, with wool felt hats, who insisted recruits use a toothbrush to clean the floor in the latrine room. Or, that the bedsheets be made so tight that dropping a quarter on the covers would cause it to bounce a few times. Or, spit-polishing the black boots until one could see a reflection. The whole boot camp episode became a demeaning experience—a high price to pay for the freedom I sought. I began to doubt I had made the right choice in leaving a comfortable home back in Southern California.

Boot camp, symbolic of an extreme orderliness and dedication to duty, represented a culture not to my liking, and I rejected it from the beginning. Fortunately, the rest of my Air Force experience turned into a more moderate and reasonable experience: a new sense of freedom and a unique combination of learning that would play a key role in my future career.

Following boot camp, my next duty station was fairly close by, at Sheppard Air Force Base in Wichita Falls, Texas. Here, along with eleven other recruits, I trained to become a computer operator at the USAF School of Applied Aerospace Sciences. The training lasted nine weeks and represented a job I had requested based on my aptitude scores. The graduation photo below shows three of the instructors and my fellow classmates. I am fourth from the left.

Graduating class at the USAF School of Applied Aerospace Sciences

The choice to learn computer operations, like my choice to learn to program in high school, proved prescient, for knowledge of computers would play an outsize role in my eventual career. For now, at the end of this training, I had to choose a military home base for the next two years. I chose an assignment in Europe and was surprised to receive one!

Computer operator became my first duty assignment at Rhein-Main Air Base in Frankfurt, Germany. Frankfurt am Main, a large city in Germany sitting on the banks of the river, Main (a tributary of the Rhein River), had over half a million people in the 1970s. The large metropolis was a critical hub for American military power in Europe during the Second World War. Rhein-Main Air Base, built next to the Frankfurt International Airport, became the busiest gateway in Europe. During the Second World War, it served as the main terminal for the Berlin Airlift. The airbase also proved indispensable during the Arab–Israeli Six-Day War. It packed a lot of history.

I arrived at the Frankfurt Airport on a hot June day; we were taken to our barracks at Rhein-Main Air Base and I quickly began adapting to the new job and environment. The base, a series of brick structures and old wooden buildings, had a bowling alley, a movie theater, and a recreational area. Not a pretty place, but practical and aging by the time I arrived. I began working the midnight shift at the computer center for the base, not expecting the disruption it would have on my biological cycles. The most vivid memory of those days is how, no matter what I did, I would inevitably get tired and fall asleep for a few minutes at around 3 a.m. every day during my shift. After the newness of the assignment wore off, the actual job proved rather boring and soon became routine. The most interesting part consisted in playing Pinochle with fellow operators, which we engaged in each night, as we waited for machines to spew out the reams of paper comprising the required reports. Occasionally, an operator would need to load the next magnetic tape onto the drive or fix the printer when the paper jammed.

During one quiet and boring night, my friend, Bob, exclaimed excitedly, "I think I'll do a numerology reading on you."

"What's that?" I asked sounding skeptical.

"Just something I do in my spare time; it will tell you of your future," he continued cagily.

"What do I have to do?" I responded unsure.

"Nothing, just give me the day, month, and year of your birthday and I'll take it from there."

So, I did. A few days later Bob handed me a seven-page typewritten report with an inscription at the top of the first page that read: Your Name Reveals Your Character; Your Birthdate is Key to Your Destiny. The analysis laid out my life from my birth year in 1953 until 2016, or approximately forty years into the future. Most surprising and intriguing, the analysis concerned the motivating force behind all my actions.

I shivered expectantly as I read:

"You want to reduce everything to its most practical level. You want your life to follow a carefully worked-out and predictable system in which discipline and hard work pay off in measured material results. You like order in everything. You are motivated by a rigid sense of duty and responsibility that applies to job, home, family, country, and the existing order of things. You are interested in workable established systems and not in speculation, innovation, or change. You want a position of respectability and financial solidity. You strive for honesty and truth, exact and unadorned. Your approach is one of a practical method which can be substantiated by fact. You are skeptical of emotional or intuitive response in both yourself and others."

I initially reacted negatively to Bob's analysis, for I did not see myself exactly as an orderly person with a rigid sense of duty. In fact, I saw myself as emotional and intuitive, the opposite of what the analysis said. I considered throwing it out many times but curiosity concerning the predictions about my future proved stronger and I kept it to see whether any would become true. These unfolding predictions surprised me many times.

C. Encountering the Greater World

Being assigned overseas in the middle of Europe came as a pleasant surprise, for it offered an opportunity to travel and explore a new continent. Traveling, as Uncle Joe had repeated over and over, is another type of learning, recalling his many adventures in the Merchant Marine. I had been skeptical regarding the veracity of his stories, but now I found myself in the middle of one, and his stories gained a bit of credibility.

I traveled by train and bus throughout many countries in Europe, including Italy, Spain, Austria, Monaco, Germany, and France. Then, after buying a cheap, brown VW bug, I made my way around in style! The architectural forms and artwork in different countries appealed to me. The first time I visited Paris, its magnificence overwhelmed me. Everywhere I looked I saw beauty, whether in the ornate buildings, monuments, and most impressively its bridges I traveled on down the Seine River. I saw it in the stunning views of Notre Dame and its French Gothic architecture as seen from the river. This only minimally prepared me for the spiritual encounter I had while standing in front of this beautiful cathedral considering its history and symbolic representation of Catholicism. Going inside felt as if I had entered the Heaven of my catechism. I literally experienced my soul reaching out to the Divine as I looked up at the tall ceiling and at the altar, flanked by the glorious colors of the stained-glass windows.

Whether in Notre Dame or in St. Peter's in Rome, or Il Duomo in Florence, I reacted strongly to these sacred and inspiring places, not only as works of art but for their ability to capture the sense of humanity reaching toward the heavens as supplicants, but also in strength and in celebration.

I remember strolling through downtown Frankfurt one day and spontaneously deciding to enter a gallery. The paintings on display attracted me as they were remarkable for the lighting each displayed, whether on a human figure or objects in a room. All the paintings exhibited a combination of ethereal and real light, gold with yellowish-greenish tints, like the light from a candle, yet like nothing I had ever seen before. I stared and stared, and like a magnet, they drew me closer to the images in front of me. One, a self-portrait of the artist as a young man, stood out. It exhibited a kind of translucent effect on the face, as if the light originated from the inside and spoke of divine nature.

Rembrandt—Self-Portrait with a Feathered Beret

I lost track of time enthralled by the beauty of the light. I soon discovered I had walked into the largest collection of Rembrandt paintings touring the continent. Considered the greatest visual artist in the history of art, Rembrandt's light and I just had a fascinating encounter. I would never forget it.

Similar experiences awaited me with the different foods, languages, the general culture, and day-to-day behavior of people. Above all, I found the people, objects, and circumstances friendlier, more orderly, and organized than in the States. Public transportation alone proved impressive everywhere I visited, whether in Germany or the Netherlands, especially in the timeliness of buses and trains. A bus scheduled to arrive at 5:30 p.m. would be there at 5:30 p.m. every day. The experience proved far different from the States where I had given up riding buses because of their unreliability.

If timeliness were not enough, the buses, trains, and especially the city streets, were always clean throughout most of Europe. There were exceptions, but the general sense that Europeans considered their environment important permeated the air. In the 1970s, the sense of caring for nature and the environment existed only in certain places in the United

States and not in the general population. The other appealing factor, which struck me as soon as I arrived, involved how fashionable and well-dressed Europeans were. I remember commenting to a friend how good everyone looked, especially those older than me, as if always in their Sunday best. I had gotten used to the sloppiness and casual dressing style of most Americans, so the contrast stood out.

Being in the air force provided an opportunity to encounter an openness and welcoming attitude that made me experience greater acceptance by others. This contrasted significantly with my encounters during middle school and high school in the United States. The manner in which Europeans responded to me as a Hispanic person proved quite intriguing. I did not have any expectations when I first arrived in Europe and frankly had not considered it.

One night, a few months after my arrival, two air force friends and I went out to a section in Frankfurt called Sachsenhausen, a district with many restaurants, bars, and nightclubs along the Main River. We entered a noisy nightclub and settled down at a table to have drinks and listen to the blaring rock music. At a table next to us were a group of three girls, likely doing what we were doing—enjoying the weekend. I remember saying hello and soon enough we were all at the same table talking and drinking.

The girl I paired up with struck me as the most beautiful girl I had ever seen. Hannah turned out to be from Austria, in her twenties and visiting friends in Germany. Someone had told me of the multi-language abilities of many Europeans. Here, to my amazement, I faced a person who knew not only perfect English but perfect Spanish along with her native German. I felt in the presence of a higher and more sophisticated species of humans.

My typical behavior in the States was to be intimidated when faced with pretty girls, shy about approaching them, talking to them, let alone asking them to dance or on dates. Hannah's openness, smile, and curiosity made me forget my shyness. We talked effortlessly for a long while. I did not realize my attraction until the following day. At that moment, I felt alive since a special person had noticed me. The novel experience surprised me. Unfortunately, Hannah headed back to Austria the following day and so we did not meet again. But, in her presence, I felt real and interesting to talk with. It was a feeling I frequently encountered when conversing with most Europeans.

It didn't take me long to recognize why such behavior felt different from my interactions with folks in the States. It seemed Europeans saw me as a real person. They were curious and interested in what I had to say and I was not invisible to them. They appeared more open and without artifice when engaging in conversation and lacked the unconscious judgmental attitudes and biases that seemed so obvious in white Americans. The immediacy of their openness and welcoming attitude made me feel more accepted. Social invisibility for Hispanics and people of color in general is not an uncommon experience in the States, and conveys a feeling of not being seen by others and therefore a perception that one does not matter. Hannah made me feel that I mattered and was worthy of interest and curiosity, and she did it by paying attention.

Feelings of invisibility, unfortunately, are still a common experience in my life even to this day and especially obvious when accompanied by my wife, who is white. Mostly, other white individuals, whether at a store, restaurant, or walking by will look and address my wife first and most times appear to ignore me. This used to bother me most at restaurants where waiters or waitresses automatically address my wife first and assume she is the responsible party. I have wondered what the signals are that I give. And the only explanation that makes sense is my slightly darker skin.

I may be wrong but the conclusion seems correct because the same behavior is less obvious when I know the other person or they are of Hispanic origin or a person of color. Such behavior bothers me less since learning, from my work as a scientist, that there is a biological predisposition in humans to respond to and mirror those in our own social, or in-group. Many factors affect how we judge others, but humans evolved to see and pay attention to those who are like us and to ignore those who are not. From an evolutionary perspective, this makes sense because our perceptual system develops to become fine-tuned and shaped by its experience. If what one experiences most of the time are folks looking like me, then our perception will specialize in perceiving them. The interesting question is why I didn't sense this bias as strongly or at all in Europe. What is it in the greater European culture improving such biases? Why is this not true in the United States?

D. Computers and Psychology

The U.S. Air Force offered me the opportunity to receive training in two areas that would play significant roles in my future career. One involved training in programming and systems analysis, namely, learning the ins and outs of computers, while the other involved training in psychology, or learning the ins and outs of human behavior. In Germany and on my return to the States to complete military service, I finished the undergraduate career in psychology begun at UCLA three years earlier.

The University of Maryland offers a multitude of courses for the military overseas. I took advantage of those opportunities and completed several of the courses, first in Germany and then at the Pentagon, my next duty station. High on my list in Germany had been Art Appreciation courses involving visits to local museums and galleries to see and study great works of art. This interest precipitated the encounter with Rembrandt in Frankfurt. Art Appreciation courses appealed to me because of their careful analysis of artwork. The attempt to gain insight into the mind of the artist itself provided a greater aesthetic appreciation of the work itself. I came to understand that to appreciate art, it is necessary to put oneself in the shoes of the artist and to understand the beauty of the piece from the inside out. One has to become the artist to gain such an aesthetic insight.

In retrospect, while engaged in concrete intellectual work as a computer geek during my day job, which was a left-brain exercise, I sought abstract and right-brain stimulation in my art education during off hours. Not unexpectedly during my two years in Germany, and because of my attempts to put myself in the minds of artists, I began to concentrate on my own pubescent art skills. I took an interest in and began to draw in pencil and charcoal and paint in watercolors. After two years overseas, I had accumulated a reasonable collection of drawings and paintings, most which were adequate and a couple I thought were good.

After the two years overseas, the military assignment came to return to the States and work at the Pentagon in Washington D.C. The assignment struck me as a dream job, as the Pentagon represented the highest level of control and power in the U.S. military. It felt prestigious and an honor to serve in such a place, an external validation of my innate talents, I thought. In Washington D.C., my assignment was at the Air Force Data Services Center, responsible for processing the Department of Defense and Secretary of Defense budgets. The work required a top-secret clearance, so I had to go through this process, which took the FBI six months to complete. During the delay, a higher authority decided I needed to switch duties from computer operations to a systems programmer/analyst. I don't recall the exact reason for the change. Perhaps they saw my potential or maybe the need for analysts had grown. The switch required more education and an elevation of responsibilities. This attracted me and I went along.

The air force spent a large amount of money training me to be a systems analyst. One memorable series of seminars I attended took place in Chicago over the course of a week. I flew from Washington D.C. to Chicago in the middle of winter to complete the classes. As adapted to the cold weather in Washington as I had become, such exposure did not adequately prepare me for what awaited me in the Windy City. I have never been so cold in my life. The only time I left the warmth of my hotel room or the seminar room involved crossing the bridge connecting the two to attend class. Crossing the bridge became a metaphor for the many bridges I would cross the rest of my life calling for change. I know wearing the right clothing would have forestalled the fearsome and the penetratingly cold wind greeting me on these short walks. I completed the courses and training and performed the analyst role the rest of my time in the service, even earning an air force commendation medal for meritorious service in this role.

While at the Pentagon and completing my military service, I finished my B.S. in Psychology from the University of Maryland, University College, in 1978. As a systems analyst, I had learned a considerable amount regarding computers, their internal organization, general principles of operation, and programming languages, making them functional. As a psychology major, I learned about human behavior, from reflexes to cognitive operations, from evolution to development, and about basic principles of human action. At the end of my time at the Pentagon, I had no inkling that these two worlds would come together seamlessly in my future academic career.

E. The Door to Academia

When one door closes, another one opens. To complete the B.S. in Psychology while still in the military, I took a military sociology class at the Pentagon. I enjoyed the class and thought had performed well. At the end of finals, the instructor of the class approached me and nonchalantly whispered, "Jaime, I just want to tell you I enjoyed your written analyses of the topics we've discussed and think you have academic potential."

I assumed he meant I had done well in the final, so I said, "Thank you. I enjoyed your class."

"Actually," he continued, "I want you to consider graduate school. I think you can handle it."

His unexpected comment left me speechless.

"If you need a letter of recommendation, I would be happy to write one," he continued.

I stuttered, "What do I need a letter for?" My naiveté regarding graduate school and the application process probably gave him pause.

But he gave me an explanation. "They require at least three letters from folks who know you, usually academics who evaluate your potential for grad school. I'm willing to write such a letter if you ever apply."

I had not contemplated graduate school, which in reality I knew nothing about. Yet, this small act of kindness from a relative stranger unexpectedly opened up a world of possibilities unknown to me. Soon afterwards, I would follow his advice. I will always be grateful for his action, for in a few words, a relative stranger changed the trajectory of my life. In retrospect, I see this as one of many turning points over which I exerted little control but now realize may not have been accidental at all.

Staying in the military as a career had been an option because of the stimulating analyst work and the health and other benefits the air force provided, which were unsurpassed. Unfortunately, exposure to life at the Pentagon short-circuited those thoughts. Nothing bothered me more than the protocol requiring everything in sight be classified as secret or even top secret. I could not see any reasonable justification. Part of what bothered me concerned the immense bureaucracy this classification system created. The public had a right to much of this information so voters could have a better basis for judging whether their military performed as effectively as the image it projected. Classifying much of this material kept information from the public and made the military less accountable to the American people.

More insidious and bothersome were the expenditures on equipment and even entire computer systems to have a backup should the main computer go down. Unfortunately, the protocol required a backup to the backup. We could have applied the millions of dollars wasted in this senseless directive to more specific needs, such as raising the salary of the airmen who carried out the work. This early sign of my progressive attitudes would come to characterize my politics. Thus, the prestige and excitement of working at the Pentagon did not lessen the impact such bureaucratic waste and unprofessionalism had in discouraging and dissuading me from staying. In 1978, I left the air force after serving in the military for five years.

CHAPTER TWO

Marriage—Forged in Fire

I met a girl of my dreams and of my reality.
It was love at first sight and many sights to love.
Letting go of the old was heartbreaking,
Touching the new was frightening.

Elizabeth Mary Meinholz

A. Building an Adult Life

I met Elizabeth (Liz) Mary Meinholz in 1976 while stationed at Fort Myer Army Base in Arlington, Virginia, and assigned to work at the Pentagon in

Washington, D.C. Liz, a Wisconsin native, had come to the nation's capital to work at the State Department. Her eventual goal included working in the diplomatic core as a potential lifetime career. But she also needed to get away from a dysfunctional relationship with her mother.

Meeting Liz transformed me, for the relationship forced changes in my childish ways to more adult-like behavior. We met when my air force roommate at Fort Myer invited me to a party Liz attended. He had been dating Liz's roommate, but the invitation meant to get me out of the barracks and meet new people. He did not intend to get me and Liz together, for Liz already had a boyfriend back in Wisconsin, and others persistently pursuing her in Washington. Liz and I discovered many similar interests during the party: writing, nature walks, education, philosophy, and religion. We talked nonstop for the duration of the party. Her obvious intelligence, a sweetness she exuded from her entire body, her smile, and a kind of untainted and innocent sense of aliveness were alluring. By the end, I felt a strong attraction.

Soon thereafter, we started dating. The first time I picked her up on a date, the weather had turned chilly. I remember standing at the opened door to her apartment in Arlington, Virginia, while waiting and shivering. I saw her coming down the stairs, a striking girl, with long blond hair and a kind and generous smile. She seemed to descend in slow motion. I could not take my eyes off of her, and when she said hello, I fell in love. Then, on our fourth date, we had gone to see a movie. Until then, I had been anxious and unsure concerning holding her hand. As we walked into the old and musky movie theatre, I felt her reach out and gently grab my right hand. Calm and ecstatic, the moment felt delicious. I don't remember the movie we saw, I only remember the feeling of her soft hand in mine. From then on, we always held hands.

Our wedding took place on June 18, 1977, a few days after I turned twenty-four years old and a year before leaving the military. Dave Fontenot and Don Reese, my buddies from the air force, served as best men. Liz had her best friend from Eau Claire, Sherry Olson, and Joelle Lira, her room-mate, as bridesmaids. Getting married represented a time-tested journey to build a life as an adult—a journey leading me into the fire of a forge, causing me to change in basic and unexpected ways.

B. A Growing Desire for Change

Getting married precipitated what had become inevitable, making a choice regarding leaving or staying in the Catholic Church. We had both grown distant from this form of Christianity. In Liz's case, her search for under-standing and meaning had led her to study the History of World Religions at George Washington University's Graduate School of Arts and Sciences. In the process of her studies, she encountered biblical and nonbiblical schol-arship questioning many of the veracities of Catholic dogma. The ground on which she had formed her set of beliefs became rattled and unstable.

For me, the reasons for questioning my religion were more personal and intuitive. The Unitarian-Universalist church in Arlington, Virginia, a liberal church focused on social outreach, provided a better fit. The time had not yet arrived for us to reject Christianity just the less progressive teachings, such as its monopoly on truth. Unitarians believe no one person or organization has a monopoly on truth, and one should therefore respect other religions and points of view. The right of people to hold alternative beliefs resonated as a more truthful approximation to what both Liz and I believed. When one studies other religions, such as Hinduism, Buddhism, Islam, and Taoism, one recognizes they have also tapped into a source of undeniable Divine Wisdom.

Equally attractive was the Unitarian belief in the moral authority, though not necessarily the divinity of Jesus. The divinity of Jesus had been a difficult issue for me, which I had questioned. How could there be only one son of God, I wondered? Didn't God create us all? Were we not made in His image? What does it mean if not that we are part of Him? And, if Jesus is not unique, what are the implications?

Liz's parents reacted badly when they heard of our decision to leave the Catholic Church and to get married in a different church. Their desire had been to have the marriage be conducted by the Roman Catholic chaplain at the Fort Myer Memorial Chapel. Their deep concern and grief flowed from their religious responsibility as parental custodians of her soul. They wished that their only daughter marry in the only church and tradition they had known, the Roman Catholic tradition. They pleaded, asked the chaplain to speak to us, and eventually threatened to not pay for the wedding and disown Liz if she married me, and especially if she rejected her Catholic upbringing. They saw no greater sin than a "fallen-away Catholic" and considered it a failure and a disgrace to have such a thing happen in their family.

We held firm to our beliefs and announced our marriage at the Unitarian Universalist (UU) Church of Arlington, Virginia. To keep inconvenient questions from Liz's family at a minimum, her mother carefully concocted a story. She assured them that the name of the church referred to St. Unitarian, a nonexistent Catholic saint. She saw it as the only way to save face. Liz and I married in the old UU Arlington Church. Her parents came to the wedding, did not disown Liz, but did not forget the whole episode. Indeed, they visited us in Arlington every Easter for many years so that we could all attend Easter Sunday Mass. For them, this represented their last attempt to save Liz (and me) from being excommunicated and eternal damnation.

C. Acknowledging Personality Differences

I left the air force in 1978, a year following my marriage to Liz. A former colonel in the air force had recruited me to move to Florida and work as a systems programmer/analyst for Miami-Dade County and their 911 system. Moving to Miami during the drug wars of the 1980s proved ominous. I had driven down from Washington D.C. to Miami on my own in my orange VW bug, the only car I trusted, while Liz completed her Master of Arts in History of World Religions at George Washington University.

When she finally moved to join me a year later, we settled in a small apartment in the Kendall area of Miami. Kendall, a relatively new middle-class section of the city, had a large shopping mall nearby.

With thoughts of faith and questions regarding religion front and center because of getting married, my interest in spiritual matters intensified and revealed a growing sense I needed to attend. One summer night, Liz and I made our way to a pizza joint at the Dadeland Mall for dinner. Like we had done many times before, we finished the meal and returned home. While watching the 11 p.m. news, a TV crew reported that half an hour after we had departed, an armed man had burst into the pizza place with a machine gun and sprayed it, killing at least one person. The hit appeared to be drug-related. It was not the only close call we experienced in Miami.

I could not help but think Fate was intervening on our behalf to keep us safe. I began to see the magical realism of my childhood, adolescence, and young adulthood years, which I had appreciated yet taken for granted, as a feature of my life I needed and now wanted to explore. This incident provided the impetus I needed to cut the last frayed attachment to my religion and to focus more on my growing spirituality. I recall this as an early recognition of a growing desire for a more conscious and meaningful spiritual exploration.

Living and working in Miami proved interesting in a new kind of way. The daily life of the city brought recent and exciting happenings almost nonstop. Just as important to us as a young married couple was the remunerative aspect of working for the local government. As a supervisor of the programming group for Miami-Dade County, I enjoyed the salary. Many Cuban-Americans worked for the county, including those who would become my close friends. As a result, I benefitted by practicing Spanish and slowly gaining a Cuban accent.

Liz and I had a happy life. We had many friends, colleagues, and a good social and intellectual life. We joined the local Unitarian Universalist

Congregation of Miami, helped organize dinner discussions, and taught religious education classes on Sunday. Teaching these classes proved to be a unique experience, for doing them together revealed our different attitudes toward children. As much common interests as we had discovered during our dating phase, Liz and I began to notice and experience the many subtle, different ways we saw life. There were personality differences magnified by the closeness of our relationship, making the fire of the marriage forge grow increasingly hotter.

The first religious education classes we taught at the Unitarian Universalist Congregation were based on the Haunting House Curriculum. It was meant to teach children about being at home with the self and in the world. In our first class, we had ten rambunctious six- to ten-year-old kids who attended the one-hour class while their parents took part in Sunday services. Liz and I had agreed on several lessons we would implement involving several work assignments, with each of us responsible for half of them. I recall being the one responsible for the lesson on building a home out of cardboard boxes and then using it to reflect on what makes a home and a family.

When it came my turn to teach, I noticed how dispirited, inattentive, and itching to run and play the children were, so I decided a bit of running around might burn up energy before we got started. Liz did not react well when the shouting, yelling, and running around got out of hand. And it got out of control, for the group had its own momentum once it started. After the running, which may have lasted only a minute, the children seemed more interested in doing the cardboard exercise, so it convinced me the exercise had worked. I would argue that a bit of logic existed in my madness.

In contrast, all of Liz's assignments required the children to sit quietly at their desks and work on the assignment. "Let them get up and walk around a bit," I insisted. But she would have none of it. We complemented each other, a kind of yin and yang—while driving the other to frustration.

Liz voiced her displeasure at my differing attitudes with children and other things once we got home and in private. I didn't blame her for feeling upset when the children ran around, but hard as I tried to get her to see the logic of it, she would not admit it. We compartmentalized these differences to get along, but the cumulative effect only got noticeable, for every once in a while, the differences created conflict.

D. Letting Go of Childish Ways

Nico Belo has written a short column in the Splinter of Wisdom blog in 2019 titled: "Marriage: Behind the Fairy Tale Hides the Fire that Burns the Frenzy of the Ego." The piece aptly describes my view of marriage during our time in Miami and thereafter, with me playing the role of a naïve and unaware individual, not cognizant of the meaning of marriage, or how to treat my life partner correctly to develop a better relationship. Marriage uncovered behaviors I had not displayed previously and which tested the limits of our connection. I remember one time when my parents had come to Miami to visit and Liz and I spent the day showing them the city. I had enjoyed the visit and the traveling around, but now we headed home alone, and her face revealed anger.

"What's wrong?" I asked. "Why the long face?" She didn't respond right away, a clue to the depth of her anger. "Didn't you have a good time?" I inquired.

"You spent the whole day ignoring me," she responded in a controlled voice. I didn't know what she meant until she went on. "You never translated everything your parents said, and I felt left out."

As we got home, I could sense the anger rising in me, for I thought I had done enough translation to keep everyone happy. True, there were times I hadn't translated, but translating is difficult to maintain during a rapid, ongoing conversation. "What do you mean?" I asked in a loud voice. "I translated for you."

"No, you didn't, and you know it," she answered back just as loudly. "Remember that bit regarding visiting Disney World? You didn't tell me exactly what they said," she went on. They had invited us to go with them to visit Disney World, but I knew Liz would not want to go and so had chosen not to translate.

"I wanted to spare you from it," I told her a bit meekly.

But she wouldn't have any of it. "You should translate and let me worry how I respond."

I raised my voice in anger and shouted, "Why don't you learn Spanish and then we wouldn't have these problems."

"You're really a piece of work," she replied. "I would talk to them directly without your help if I could."

I headed for the door, slammed it loudly and left. After driving around the city for an hour, I returned, unsure of how to face Liz and admit my mistake. Following several similar episodes, the futility of my actions became clear, for they were nothing but a child's tantrum in an adult and concerning inconsequential matters. For one, I realized I always returned home and apologized—so, I asked myself, "Why leave to begin with?" "And why do I have to slam the door each time?" I reasoned it would be more efficient and effective in the long run if I stayed and talked things out, calmly confronting the issue, which is what Liz wanted to do, anyway. Teaching me how to be a real adult took additional episodes of such temper tantrums before I finally learned to expect them and disarm the volatility.

Liz and I also argued, although a lot less, about children. From the beginning, Liz had been forthright she did not want children for a variety of reasons. "I just don't have the mothering instinct," she would say. I could not hear and understand her argument, for my culture and family saw children as the reason for marriage. For Latinos, children are the inevitable consequence of a man and a woman marrying. Mom constantly reinforced this expectation with her incessant questioning. "Cuando vienen los bebitos?" she would ask, "When are the babies coming?" I would raise the issue with Liz and fruitless and pointless arguments followed, until my eyes finally opened. I conceded the argument to Liz because my desire seemed to originate more in the expectation than in the reality of what I wanted. While briefly disappointed, I did not regret my decision. Liz had forced me to face a deeply rooted belief regarding having children, which made me realize the desire did not originate from me but from external sources, familial and cultural expectations.

Liz influenced me to become more self-reflective, aware, and overall a better person. For the next twenty-five years, we followed a similar script, with Liz providing the fire to the forge and assuming a civilizing and moderating influence over me. Many times, this occurred at the expense of her own happiness, as when she accompanied me on a visit to Honduras. It thrilled my parents and me since it would be her first time there.

On the third day of our visit, however, Liz whispered, "I don't feel well. I think I will be sick." We had been careful not to drink tap water only bottled water, but she began experiencing digestive problems. I bought Pepto-Bismol and another anti-diarrhea medication but she did not respond to them.

"I think you should rest and get better." I tried to reassure her she would improve quickly.

"Where are you going?" she asked me one morning as I headed out to visit my sisters.

"We're visiting the family," I responded. "I'll be back soon. Do you have everything you need?"

"Why don't you stay and let your parents go by themselves?" she pleaded.

"I have to see my sisters. I haven't seen them in two years. It's why we came," I replied.

"But I get bored here. I can't watch TV since I don't understand it. Please stay and keep me company," she said tearfully.

"I can't," I said gruffly. "I'll be back as soon as I can."

I now realize how callous, uncaring, unloving, and childish it must have seemed to her. I should have stayed at her side, kept her company, kept her spirits up. It would have been the caring, loving, and adult behavior. Liz was furious, and rightly so, for a long time after.

Miami became the foundry from which emerged a changed me. For one, my temper became less volatile and more controlled. I tried to be more sensitive to Liz's needs and to her demands, especially in doing more housework. Besides these challenges in the marriage, I also faced the first suicide of a friend and co-worker.

Guy Modugno, a talented, gay, and troubled young programmer, had the uncanny ability to always find the programming problems typically besetting the Miami-Dade 911 system. He had become an indispensable diagnostician for maintaining the system functioning twenty-four–seven. Because of his alacrity, Guy reminded me of an intense yellow flower in the middle of a monotone green background. Everyone liked him and he reciprocated. The futility, helpless feelings, and nonstop thoughts regarding his suicide created an endless loop of regrets in my head. To think I could have done more to recognize, help, or prevent whatever monster consumed Guy, created painful emotions.

After much consideration and spinning of tires on these thoughts, I reached a point where I could set aside the emotions. I concluded it was possible to have no answer to life's problems and yet be able to move on constructively. It did not mean I forgot the happy memories or the painful ones but could hold them in my heart and still continue living and working. In the deep recesses of my mind, I felt a nagging sense there had to be better answers to these problems.

E. Searching for a Deeper Spiritual Life

My work at Miami-Dade, while intellectually satisfying, became less and less fulfilling. I remember noticing one aspect of the work that most satisfied me. It occurred during team meetings with the other programmers and analysts making up the group. At these meetings, we would think through problems, brainstorm, offer solutions, and anticipate potential problems. I enjoyed the camaraderie, the intellectual back and forth, and the actual conversation with other colleagues trying to find solutions to problems. Following those meetings, work consisted of sitting at a desk with a computer, either coding or monitoring the 911 system. It quickly became clear that systems analysis or computer work by itself did not satisfy me. Despite the excellent salary, working with people more than with machines gained a strong and compelling attraction, forcing me to search for alternatives.

After much thought and discussion with Liz, I returned to school to pursue Master's in Psychology. Like a moth to light, an inner vibration had drawn me to the study of psychology one more time. The compromise we agreed to hinged on me returning to work at Miami-Dade following completion of the two-year degree. Liz and my supervisor, who agreed to hold my job open, were pleased. A higher degree meant an upper management position with greater pay and benefits so the idea made sense and I went along. The letter of recommendation from the Military Sociology instructor at the Pentagon became important in facilitating my return to academia. I could not shake the feeling, though, that these life trajectories and detours, from getting married to developing a career, kept delaying my search for a certain freedom and meaningfulness I craved. I wanted freedom to follow my nascent intellectual and spiritual aspirations. I sensed these would provide a greater understanding of life, deeper satisfaction, and help me make more of a difference to others.

I attended a school with a good psychology program, away from Miami, but close enough to make returning possible. Florida Atlantic University (FAU) in Boca Raton met my requirements. Attending FAU would require moving from Miami to Boca Raton, approximately fifty miles north. The campus stood less than two miles from the Atlantic Ocean. Being close to water appealed to me. Boca Raton is the jewel of Palm Beach County and among the wealthiest communities in South

Florida. Its pristine beaches attract thousands of students from northern climates during spring break.

Liz and I rented a nice two-bedroom apartment with a pool, in the neighboring community of Deerfield Beach about four miles south of FAU. I settled down to the hard work of graduate school. Liz began her teaching career at the Pompano Beach Adult and Community School, having completed her Master's in Religion. She served as the Director of Adult Education at the Unitarian-Universalist Fellowship in Boca Raton where she taught seminars on Religion in America.

Florida is relatively flat, with few hills. The striking flatness of the FAU campus allows one to see three hundred and sixty degrees all around, helping one experience a sense of being in a clear, blue-covered bowl. I felt like the one under scrutiny from a higher being, instead of the one beginning an experimental psychology program. My feelings regarding the move included a mixture of apprehension and excitement as I launched into the required courses and research. Returning to school intensified my two growing interests—learning more about human behavior and spiritual matters.

Carlos and Loretto at their wedding

I met Carlos Comperatore, a first-year cohort, with dark, penetrating eyes and a mop of curly dark hair during orientation. We hit it off right away, as if we had known each other before. When I first shook his hand, he reminded me of my childhood friends, Pablo, Hector, and the Hernandez brothers, all rolled into one. Carlos, married to Loretto and of Argentinian descent, became my best friend at that time. During our first get-together with our wives at his apartment, Carlos brought up the subject of meditation.

"I've been practicing meditation for several years," he said in a proud tone.

"What do you do when meditating?" I asked.

He got up from the living room, went into a bedroom and came out with what looked like a fully stuffed, brown pillow. "I sit on this, it's called a zafu," he explained while showing us the roundish cushion. "Try it," he urged me.

He then showed me how to sit comfortably with a straight back and legs crossed in front. I could not completely sit in what he called the lotus position, with legs fully crossed, and could only achieve a half-lotus.

"It's fine to start that way and maybe with time learn the full lotus," he smiled.

I already felt the strain on my legs so got up quickly. "It'll take me a long time to learn how to sit," I said.

"You don't know the half of that," he quipped with a slight smile.

I began practicing sitting on a similar cushion, and Carlos and I became fellow travelers on our individual spiritual and intellectual journeys. We would sit and meditate together occasionally but mostly I learned on my own. I got feedback from Carlos and from books, but mainly learned through trial and error. In the long run, this proved to be a mistake, for I picked up many bad habits and innumerable ways to do things the wrong way. The interest in and necessity for a real spiritual teacher would not materialize for another ten years.

The anticipation of learning how to meditate properly proved more rewarding than the actual doing. My feelings of frustration and uncertainty grew slowly, in a mind thirsty for such knowledge. Meditation is a conditioning of the body and mind to deal with physical and mental stillness. This stillness, what Rodney Smith has defined as the "unequivocal resolve not to move away from where we are," does not come easily to a body accustomed to movement and flights of fancy. It would be many years before I understood there is in fact stillness inherent even in movement.

But to master meditation requires a long and gradual process performed repeatedly, like any other learned behavior. Forty years after the passion evoked during those early days of exploration, it has yet to recede. The meditation we practiced involved a particular form of mindfulness Carlos introduced me to, involving counting in and out breaths to train focused attention. That exercise would morph into sitting in silence in what Buddhists call Shikantaza, or sitting in awareness.

Mindfulness at this point meant the ability to distinguish between perception and thought or between ephemeral ideas and the arising of sensory experience. The effort involved the observation of the mind at work without making judgments, which reinforces our dependency on appearances. In a still mind, mindfulness is just awareness. For me, mindfulness practices, such as counting breaths or just sitting, were like water and fertilizer to a thirsty and dying plant. Mindfulness transformed ideas and feelings beginning to stir in me but which needed the nutrients these techniques provided. The beginning exercises tested my resolution, for my body had to adjust considerably to this new attitude. It became the orientation toward and the elixir for the elusive freedom I had craved for so long.

While I craved the spirit meditation provided, I needed to understand it at a more intellectual level.

"What books would you recommend for me to read," I asked Carlos one day while in the lab trying to get the equipment to work. "I need to know more about meditation history and philosophy, but most textbooks seem too dense and boring."

"I've got a couple I think you'll like," he replied. "I'll bring them to you tomorrow." The next day, I saw him carrying two books, which he turned over to me. "This one will give you the background and history in an easy-to-understand form," he said as he handed me a paperback titled, *The Way of Zen* by Alan Watts. "Alan is a theologian and Episcopal priest known for interpreting and popularizing Eastern philosophy for a Western audience," he informed me.

"Some Zen teachers don't think Alan truly understands Zen, but I don't agree and found his explanations interesting and insightful," Carlos continued. "This other one concerns ordinary people who've had an enlightenment experience and might help motivate your practice." He handed me another thicker hardcover book titled, *The Three Pillars of Zen* by Philip Kapleau.

"I'll start with the *Way of Zen*," I told him, "and go from there."

I did, and it took many years before I finally felt ready to read Kapleau's book. In his unique style, Alan Watts opened my heart to the perennial philosophy of universalism, that all religions, despite their surface differences, point to the same truth. I had heard a similar message in the Unitarian-Universalist theology. But, in Watts' book I found the door and pathway to Heaven, a Heaven I had not even imagined.

Most intriguing about the *Way of Zen* was its description of the role science and spirituality play in our ideas of reality. Science, it argues, demolished the bedrock ideas Western science itself had established by the middle of the twentieth century. Science had convincingly set matter as the fundamental substrate in nature and the idea that all things, including consciousness, result from material interactions. Consciousness, in this case, is the quality of sentience or awareness of internal or external existence.

In neuroscience, this perspective argues the point of view that mind is what the brain does, a byproduct of the actions of the biological machinery. Watts claimed that the twentieth century exploded with ideas regarding quantum mechanics, cubism, modern music, Freudian psychology, and other concepts. These ideas challenged the widely accepted notions of space, time, and motion, of nature and natural law, of history and social change, and of human personality.

Thus, the foundation of materialism and of our identities was questioned and shattered by the same science investigating these realities. As a result, statements like "the brain is a product of the mind" came into consideration and raised doubts. What if materialism is wrong? What is an alternative explanation? What is more real than material substance? For many scientists and intellectuals, all they could imagine as an alternative to materialism was an absence or emptiness, a great void containing absolutely nothing. Emptiness crashes with the existential longing for definition and individuation.

Before long, as Watts claimed, these attacks on foundational ideas of being, produced individuals "adrift without landmarks in a universe which more and more resembled the Buddhist principle of the 'Great Void.'" Watts argued that faced with such a possibility, the greatest wisdom of the West, its religious, philosophical, and scientific traditions did not offer much guidance to the art of living in such an empty universe. To be nothing, immaterial, stand on nothing, and having no guidance on how to proceed can be psychologically disconcerting, paralyzing, and frightening. Watts' argument resonated deeply for he seemed to describe what I considered my unmoored, drifting life, and my artless and clueless attempt at living it. While my professional life appeared stable, fulfilling, and with a future, it had become a rather confusing time spiritually. Outer appearances can deceive and I felt spiritually adrift. I suppose I was one of those looking out at an empty universe and somewhat paralyzed by the thought.

From a Buddhist perspective, the nature of this emptiness or void is much more sensible and positive. My understanding is that it is not the absence of things but a condition in which actions proceed unimpeded and unobstructed by other actions, in which all matter performs its own function unencumbered. In this way, emptiness serves as the foundation for matter to express itself naturally and perfectly. If no great void or emptiness condition existed, it might not be possible for the material world to exist and function.

Watts introduced me to this new perspective and to a "productive way of life which, for fifteen hundred years, has felt thoroughly at home in this emptiness, and which not only feels no terror in it but rather a positive delight." "At its heart," he continued, "there is in Zen a strong but completely unsentimental compassion for human beings suffering and perishing from their attempts to save themselves" in a universe they misperceive as cool and cruel. I didn't need to read anymore, for the argument had hooked me. I could not wait to further explore this new and more productive way of life. This introduction to Zen became the culmination of my interest in magical realism, the type pervading my life until then. Such thinking senses the existence of immaterial elements in the world, coupled with a sensibility to hidden meanings. I walked through the door Watts opened and never turned back. I entered a spiritual universe where I felt quite at home and found support for my intuitions of life's connectedness and caring nature.

CHAPTER THREE
Home in Science

There is what we know and what we don't.
The latter is much vaster than the former.
Within this there is what can become known,
And that which can't.

Dr. Alan Nash

A. A Meaningful Intellectual Existence

At the same moment I waked through the spiritual door Alan Watts and Zen had opened up, my return to education created another path, based on science. It allowed the seeking of truth from a different perspective. The interaction and natural antagonism between my scientific and spiritual interests were just beginning to gain momentum. Interestingly, another Alan (or the same harmonic spiritual force) opened the second door, the one leading me on the path of science.

Dr. Alan Nash (1937-2017), my advisor at FAU, encouraged me to continue my research interests started in his lab and to apply to PhD programs. Like the sociology professor at the Pentagon, Alan saw potential in my abilities and contributed to pushing me in the direction of science. A Wisconsin native, Alan had a tall and lanky academic appearance, with an easy smile and a slow Midwestern drawl. He studied neural activity during cognitive events. When I visited FAU searching for an advisor, my background as an analyst and attachment to computers made me make a beeline to the hardware, computers, and other electronic devices strewn throughout Alan's lab. He turned out to be generous with his time, patient with naïve graduate students, focused on using the brain's own electrical language to discover its truths, and willing to teach me all he knew. He became my academic advisor.

Even though Alan seemed to move and talk slower than most other faculty in the department, the time in his lab flew by. After two years of work—which seemed more like six months—I completed the Master of Arts in Experimental Psychology in1982. The thesis was titled, "The relationship between P300 elicited during a primary task and performance on a near-simultaneous secondary signal detection task." This work set in motion the tone and tenet that would follow me throughout the rest of my research career.

What I still remember vividly from those last days at FAU is Alan's kind smile and advice, as well as the overwhelming sense of anxiety and fear I felt the night before my oral defense. I literally crawled the wall as I rubbed my back against a hallway wall at home while practicing my talk. I survived the ordeal, but now a difficult choice faced me. Did I go back to my previous analyst job at the Miami-Dade or continue on this new path of science?

I sought advice from Alan and knew he would recommend continuing graduate training.

"You should apply to PhD programs in Psychology," he said. "Here is a list of good ones," he said while handing me a sheet of paper. On the paper, he had written university names like Northwestern, Wisconsin, Stanford, UCLA, and several others. "These all have strong Psych programs, especially in biological psychology, which would be a good area for your interests," he continued.

"What do you know of Neuroscience programs?" I quizzed him trying to change topics. "I've been looking at these programs and they seem attractive."

"I know nothing about Neuroscience," he responded. "Although, I don't think that's a good fit for you," he continued.

I had researched programs in psychology and neuroscience because I wanted to explore human mysteries: Why do I behave the way I do? What is it in the brain making such behavior possible? I explored the neuroscience route without knowing why. Those around me, including Alan, knew little concerning this relatively new discipline. Neuroscience turned out to be a multidisciplinary approach to the study of the brain. It was the path I wanted but did not know it. Neuroscience research includes approaches at different scales and the use of techniques from molecular to cellular and imaging of sensory, motor, and cognitive tasks. At least as far as the description went, neuroscience proved way too interesting for me to pass up.

After much consideration, I jumped into this unknown. I resolved not to return to Miami-Dade and at Alan's urging began to apply to a variety of PhD programs. I had jumped without a parachute. The decision marked a major turning point in my life. The choice between a life of poverty as a graduate student for the sake of a science career over a well-paying job as a systems analyst back in Miami struck me as short-sighted but the right one. One mitigating factor would be the opportunity to use the GI Bill I qualified for because of having served in the air force. The small amount of money would function not quite as a parachute but as a small umbrella to ease the transition. I had chosen science for I saw a lifetime of unique challenges and opportunities. The mysteries of human behavior, from an evolutionary to a developmental perspective, from individual to group actions, from automatic to controlled processes, had appealed to me more than money and more than computers.

Now I had to convince Liz of my choice. My decision appeared to hinge on weak reasoning: to know why humans act the way they do, I had to first know the substrate or neural mechanisms underlying it. I say "weak" because I did not know but sensed that to understand the complexity of human behavior, one has to understand more than the biology or psychology of human actions. I now know that social, economic, and cultural environments are equally important in how humans act and interact, as are a host of other factors. I remember thinking my rationale made sense, yet I could not help feeling it meant jumping into a deep well of the unknown without a net of any sort. Liz, not unexpectedly, reacted skeptically and wisely concerned regarding the lack of a backup plan.

"You're making such a good salary here and we can probably afford to buy a house soon. Why do you want to jeopardize all that?" she asked a bit displeased.

"I just don't feel happy doing what I'm doing," I responded apologetically. "I think I can do more, especially working with people. I'm tired of dealing only with computers."

"You should do what makes you happy," she responded, as she realized she could not deter me.

Graduate school delayed our plans and put in jeopardy the financial stability we both wanted. Her total support reflected her love and commitment to our relationship. Fortunately, letters from schools came back quickly before I changed my mind. Several programs accepted my application and invited me to visit, including programs at Northwestern, the University of Illinois at Urbana-Champaign, and the University of California, San Diego (UCSD). I chose UCSD's Neuroscience program after visiting all those places and recognizing none compared to San Diego and the beauty of the city. Since the Neuroscience program at UCSD rated among the top programs in the country, it reinforced my decision. I started as a PhD student in 1982. Liz and I made the cross-country trip from Florida in our old, orange VW bug, stopping on the way in Eau Claire, Wisconsin, to visit her parents. Two years into the program, UCSD became the number one neuroscience program in the country.

Dr. Helen J. Neville

B. From Scary Unknown to Appealing Known

My scary jump into the unknown field of scientific research turned into a slow descent with a soft landing. It confirmed the rightness of my decision. I chose Dr. Helen Neville as my PhD thesis advisor. Dr. Neville (1946–2018) is considered a most influential and visionary psychologist and neuroscientist. Her groundbreaking work includes the neural basis of language, neural plasticity, and the negative effects of poverty on the brain. At that time, she had an appointment at the Salk Institute in San Diego and with the Neuroscience program on the UCSD campus. Like Dr. Alan Nash before, Helen's generosity with her time and her intelligence and her unrelenting guidance appealed to me. She taught me to collect good data, analyze it thoroughly, and link the results to previous ones. Helen made talking to her easy, not intimidating, and always with a smile or a rejoinder to make me feel better.

Helen had been collaborating with Dr. Stephen Foote, who had an appointment in the Psychiatry Department. They were working on a monkey model of cognition. Working with animals appealed to me as a worthwhile challenge and maybe even fun. I chose to do my dissertation work with these two wonderful folks.

Dr. Stephen L. Foote

Joining Helen's research group proved to be a thrilling part of my good fortune. I remember one day sitting in her lab in one of the top floors of the Salk Institute overlooking the Pacific Ocean. The red, orange, and pink tones of a setting sunset filtered through the large glass window. I could also see two individuals lazily parasailing and braving the air currents of the La Jolla Hills. The beauty of the world and the rightness of the moment struck me like a sledgehammer. I realized how fortunate I was to be there at that precise instant exploring the mysteries of the brain with such renowned scientists and wonderful people as my mentors.

The unknown had become known, and I found it staggeringly appealing. Out of the infinite possibilities my life could have taken, why did this moment happen? And why did it feel so right? It's difficult to know whether any other set of possibilities would have felt right. The circumstances made me happy to be there doing those things. In retrospect, I sensed an intelligence far greater than myself guiding me to that moment.

C. The Alluring Landscape of Science

Walking around and exploring the new and interesting landscape of science, I came upon two alluring characters: "the blue place" and the electrical potential. Like the Sirens in Homer's *Odyssey*, they lured and beguiled me and began to relate their stories, causing me to crash my ship on their rocky coastlines. From the classes I took, I became interested in the noradrenergic (NA)-locus coeruleus (LC), or NA-LC for short. This is an evolutionarily well-preserved brain circuit in mammals centered on a small region in the depths of the brain, which contains approximately twenty thousand cells in humans, called the locus coeruleus or LC. Because it has a distinctively bluish color against the grayness of the brain, it is also known as the blue place. I found its uniqueness compelling. When activated, the small number of cells in the blue place release norepinephrine onto their target cells, which literally is the entire brain. Norepinephrine is a neurotransmitter similar to epinephrine, also known as adrenaline (therefore the adjective noradrenergic, as adrenal glands release adrenaline in the peripheral nervous system). The NA-LC system is the most extensive network in the brain. When it talks, the entire brain listens.

P300 EVOKED POTENTIAL

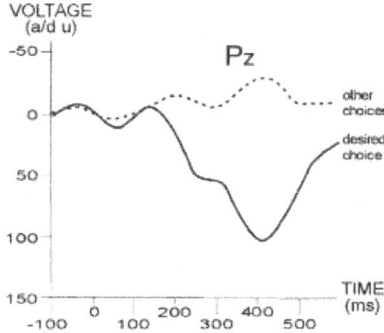

I became interested in the relationship between this blue place and an electrical potential called the P300. The brain produces the P300 approximately three hundred milliseconds after a novel or unexpected event, such as someone suddenly calling your name. The electrical brain signal is recorded as a positive voltage on the scalp. P300 events occur when the brain orients to new and unexpected things, remembers them, and establishes the meaning of those occurrences. Hundreds, if not thousands, of studies have described the properties of this distinctive cognitive event.

My dissertation work focused on the relationship between the NA-LC, an anatomically circumscribed location in the brain and an electrical event associated with high-level cognition. It was one of the first attempts to examine such a link. Problems or issues not previously addressed and which may be of relevance to a field become fodder for dissertations. This requires an extensive reading of the literature, identifying a question or set of questions not previously addressed, or at least not fully, justifying why it is important to address these unknowns, and then spelling out in detail, usually by proposing several studies. So, the specific question which received the okay from my mentors, Helen and Steve, turned on whether I could identify a neural mechanism producing a simple cognitive event? More technically, was the NA-LC necessary for the P300 to occur? Was this a significant enough idea meriting a dissertation?

In the early 1980s, when I began the project, little solid evidence existed for that kind of relationship partly because it is not an easy issue to address. To make the project workable, I first had to identify a task producing a cognitive response in humans. This led me to focus on the P300 because it is a cognitive event elicited by a simple visual- or sound-based task. The easiest task used to elicit that response is called the beep–boop task, comprising repetitive "beep" sounds presented every second and interrupted by occasional novel "boop" sounds. Second, I had to identify an easily recorded and measured biological marker of this response to novel events. The P300 is easily recorded on the scalp of human subjects by recording the electroencephalogram (EEG) while subjects listen to the beep–boop task. It responds more when the event they perceive is novel or relevant. Third, I had to show that a similar cognitive event occurs in an animal using a similar task. This is what scientists call developing an animal model. We chose monkeys because of their similarities to humans. These animals would listen to the beep–boop task while I recorded their scalp EEG. And finally, I had to determine the neural systems involved in the production of the P300 event in the monkey. This last part by itself would involve several studies. I realized there were hundreds of possible neural mechanisms, so a better way to approach the problem was to recognize that certain mechanisms are more likely to be involved than others. After reading the literature, I knew the NA system of the brain produced startle responses and showed responsiveness to novelty. Likewise, as this system originated in the LC or blue place, I assumed this would be a good place to start the search. In this way, I conceived the various steps in my dissertation work.

The training and discipline I received in the PhD program helped me deal effectively with the hard work and negativity, including stress, while keeping my eyes on the positive. I began to recognize and appreciate the value of the discipline Grandma Livia instilled in me. She had taught me to be persistent in doing work; that rewards may not come for a long time; to be patient in delaying gratification; and finally, to do the best in everything I did. She had prepared me for my life in graduate school and science.

D. Animals That Shaped My Life

The animals required for my dissertation work were monkeys and this expertise reflected Steve Foote's forte. Steve had graduated from the Massachusetts Institute of Technology (MIT) and had joined, as a junior colleague, Dr. Floyd Bloom's Neuropharmacology Laboratory at the Salk Institute and at Scripps Research Clinic. Steve later joined the Psychiatry Department at UCSD. I met Steve at Floyd Bloom's regular lab meetings, which were always on Wednesdays and were called Star Treks. These exciting and meaningful discussions took me on unexpected and fascinating scientific adventures, just like the TV series of my youth, as various lab members presented their latest findings. Steve, along with Floyd and others, had been studying a special class of neurotransmitters called the monoamines, a set of neurochemicals, including norepinephrine, that provide the means of communication across synaptic gaps. These neurotransmitters are involved in producing several general behaviors we all exhibit, including vigilance, arousal, attention, memory processes, and the detection of novelty.

Saimiri sciureus or squirrel monkey

I remember one day visiting Steve in his lab at the Salk Institute and hearing bird chirps coming from the experimental room. I looked around but couldn't see any birds and soon realized the sounds were coming from a recording device being played through speakers and directed at a small cage. I could distinctly hear: chirp–chirp–chirp–chirp–squawk–chirp–chirp–squawk, and so on. I remember that on hearing the squawk sound in between the chirp sounds, I could experience my brain responding differently, a bit of a startle response. As I approached the cage, I could see a small monkey, the size of a large cat, sitting in a plexiglass chair. The monkey had the cutest round face, short fur, black at the shoulders and yellowish-orange on its back and extremities, and a rather long tail.

The monkey, which I learned was a squirrel monkey—or technically a *Saimiri sciureus*—is a new-world species native to the tropical forests of Central and South America. While we were both natives of Central America, this was the first one I'd ever seen. The monkey seemed comfortable in the chair looking straight ahead. He pulled a lever with his right hand whenever he heard the squawk sound. This intrigued me and I wanted to ask questions of Steve who stood nearby. But Steve put his right index finger over his mouth in a sign I interpreted to mean "keep silent." For thirty minutes, the monkey listened to the frequent chirp sounds and the occasional squawk sound for which he pressed the lever. When the monkey made a correct press, juice flowed through a small tube sitting near his mouth which he drank eagerly. At the end of the session, Steve told me this was an active auditory task, with a monkey trained for many months to respond to the novel squawk sound. The hope was that this would get its brain to elicit a P300 event.

"When the brain hears repetitive sounds, such as the chirps, it habituates and responds less and less to those sounds. But when it hears a novel sound like the squawk, which occurs 10% of the time, the brain startles and emits this large electrical pattern we record as the P300. This is a variation of the classic beep–boop task," Steve explained.

"Yeah, I could feel my brain respond to the squawk sound," I said.

"It's likely the squawk sound elicited the same response in you as it did in the monkey," Steve responded.

"What does it all mean? Why are you doing this?" I asked.

"We are trying to see if monkeys exhibit P300s like humans do to novel events. If we can show they are similar events, it will allow us to study the neural basis of the response in these monkeys and hopefully generalize to humans."

"That's cool. But why is it important?"

"It can begin to tell us the neural basis of a cognitive event. In this case the response to novelty. Then, if we know where in the brain it happens and why it happens, we may help individuals who have a disorder associated with this mechanism."

"What do you mean a disorder of this mechanism?" I asked quizzically.

"There are clinical patients who don't respond to novelty like you and I," Steve explained.

"In fact, there are some folks who overreact or underreact compared to the normal population of humans. We could help such an oversensitivity or under-sensitivity if we know what areas of the brain is involved," he responded.

"I like what you are doing and think I want to work on this project," I announced excitedly before I realized I should have asked if he needed graduate student help with the work. He did! In no time, this became the basis for my dissertation.

Steve had become an expert on the LC (the blue place) and had perfected ways to record brain electrical patterns inside the brain in awake, behaving monkeys as they performed the beep–boop tasks. It was not an easy procedure! To do that requires a technique called single-unit electrophysiology. This means inserting a small, thin, metal recording device, called an electrode, into the brain slowly until the right place is located. Electrical activity is then recorded as the cell becomes active. Prior to Steve and others, single-unit studies required monkeys be anesthetized, that is they were essentially asleep or nonresponsive. But anesthetized animals limit what one can study.

Steve, along with other scientists, developed methods for single-unit recordings in awake, behaving monkeys. This meant one could study behaviors only possible in an awake state, allowing someone like me to study cognition. Steve's expertise also extended to the use of drugs injected inside the brain to disrupt operations in brain circuits to study their function. His interest in cognition, his expertise in all areas of animal work, his collaboration with Helen, and his inimitable humor and sharp wit attracted me and we ended up working well together. Like most good mentors, both Helen and Steve taught me as much about life as the process of research. My observation of their behavior in response to problems was part of the lessons.

One afternoon I walked into Steve's office quite upset. We were at the end stages of putting together a publication in which Helen, Steve, and I would be co-authors. I had seen Helen that morning to review our last-minute data analysis, and she expressed skepticism regarding my interpretation. She asked me to redo the analysis. I left irritated and angry, for it meant she didn't trust the results and a month or more of delaying what I knew needed no correction. I wanted Steve's perspective on the issue.

"Next time don't go over these results with Helen," Steve advised, which took me by surprise. "She doesn't understand single-unit physiology. Let her review the EEG data but let me decide about the single-unit data," he continued with a smile.

I felt a wave of relief, for I understood the implication. I would not have to redo the analysis. I learned more in that short interaction than in most of the classes I had taken. For it encouraged me to stand my ground, even in the face of an authority figure, especially when you are confident in your decision. Steve convinced Helen about the correctness of my analysis and the study moved quickly to publication. I remember Steve's smile throughout the incident.

The work I wanted to do to study the blue place and the electrical P300 potential required working with animals. This immediately put me at odds with my growing concerns about the ethics of doing that. Working with monkeys became fraught with questions regarding the morality of using them for research. Most times, especially if the interest is to study behavior, animals are trained to perform an action, and scientists then study the action. In those cases, an animal may live for a long time doing many such behavioral studies.

Other studies, like those I conducted, require the examination of the brain in order to know where in the brain the understanding of a novel event occurs. And, if one knows the area, what other areas connect to it? This meant humanely euthanizing the animal subjects (euthanasia being a scientific and neutral term for sacrificing the animal for the sake of scientific research) to examine the brain. There are protocols to follow, making sure animals don't suffer when this happens. For instance, animals are first anesthetized or put to sleep. But having to euthanize the monkeys at the end of my studies made the investigations especially difficult and distressing.

I wanted to be a scientist and my rational mind convinced me humans have an inherent need to know. I convinced myself that the greater good of humanity made vivisection necessary, and that our human needs supersede animal rights. I applied the same rationale for why I ate animal meat and why my needs superseded theirs. These rationalizations began to fray when they collided with my growing interest and understanding of Buddhism.

While human needs are real, new technology can get the same results without sacrificing animals. Alternatives like computer simulation evolved hand-in-hand with the rapid growth of the computer in the 1980s, and can provide insights into the computations necessary for how to move an arm, or make sounds like vocal cords. Likewise, using more primitive organisms, like proteins, viruses, or even mice and rats, offer the prospect of a good alternative to answer questions concerning simple behaviors. The question is, how do we study complex behaviors when only animals like monkeys can produce them? These include teaching a young infant to play with playmates, fight off an intruder, understand the intent of another monkey when it looks up and gives the danger signal, or how to use sticks to get food from an anthill, and so on.

Regardless of my struggle with these issues, I continued the research. Immediately, I faced the question of whether to sacrifice a monkey because of poor health. The ethical dilemma arose because a squirrel monkey had contracted an illness and the veterinarian did not know how to treat it. The options included letting the monkey die, which might take a long time, or sacrifice the animal immediately. The decision weighed on me. In my reading and understanding of Buddhism, animal experimentation is considered morally wrong if the animal concerned might come to any harm. However, Buddhists acknowledge the value of animal experiments in human health. Thus, I opted to sacrifice the monkey to minimize its suffering.

Another similar situation arose involving a different and more developed and intelligent monkey species. I completed my studies using macaque monkeys, in addition to squirrel monkeys, and kept two of the macaques to the end hoping another researcher would use them for additional studies. Unfortunately, that option did not materialize, and I had no choice but to euthanize them. This time, the only reason involved having to move on to other things and having no need for the animals. Like the hummingbird of my early youth, which I had killed unintentionally as a four-year-old, I saw myself as the prime cause of the unnecessary deaths of these monkeys. The decision made me less willing to pursue this kind of work. I did not want to kill unnecessarily, and even the justification for doing scientific work as a necessity for human well-being had lost its sway.

E. The Potential for Unethical Behavior

Aside from the ethical questions of using animals in research, I crashed head-on into a subtler but just as potentially damaging behavior. One that can erode a fundamental pillar of science: the veracity of data. Getting a PhD requires hard work. The process involves classes during the first two years, accompanied by endless hours in the lab collecting and analyzing data. My training required I check my results with two advisors, and more likely had to redo the analyses more than most. One day, which blurred with many other days, I found myself at Helen Neville's lab at the Salk Institute working on EEG data analysis. The clock marked midnight. After endless hours sitting at a computer, collecting and cleaning up numbers representing brain electrical activity, I set up to run the statistic program that would tell me if I had significant results. When I say "clean up" numbers I mean to apply statistically accepted methods to remove things like outliers, or data points several standard deviations from the mean, and to replace them with the average of the clean data. Unfortunately, after these procedures, the numbers came back and did not show significance.

My disappointment forced a muted utterance I can't repeat as I watched months of work disappearing down the metaphorical drain. I sat in stunned silence for many seconds until a thought occurred to me. How much would the numbers have to change to get significance? The ease of making such changes with no one the wiser struck me as workable yet frightening. Tired and alone in the lab in the middle of the night, I considered it. Reporting a significant result would guarantee publication of this work and the beginning of making a name for myself. I saw temptation staring me in the eye and could sense the dangerous road ahead. After what seemed like interminable minutes, but were only a few seconds, an even more powerful thought crossed my mind: doing that would be wrong!

The thought cleared away the developing cobwebs. And in a flash, made me realize how personally unethical and wrong the manipulation of data would be. I felt ashamed I had even considered the possibility. I swore I would never think of doing it again. For a long time, I wondered where the strength to overcome the tempting thoughts came from. Its source seemed to be the same spiritual energy guiding and protecting me. Even now, as I write this, a feeling of gratitude overwhelms me. For even though temptation made its appearance several other times during this phase of my work, the initial resolution had strengthened my resolve, and I never broke it.

Professional journals withdraw publications occasionally because researchers are found to have manipulated scientific data. This represents a miniscule part of the totality of the research and publication taking place. Yet, purposeful falsification of data would undo a basic pillar of science: the trust we place on those who carry out the enterprise and the confidence we have on the results. This issue keeps me up at night, knowing how easy it is to manipulate data and how many people may fall prey to temptation. We have no way of knowing how widespread it is. If it is, then the bedrock of science is more unstable than we realize.

Required classes on ethics and ethical conduct did not exist for graduate students in the 1980s. This has changed. Today all students, from undergraduates to postdoctoral, must take such courses. The National Institutes of Health requires students and faculty to receive training in ethical behavior, especially when involved in training grants. While the field recognizes the frailty of humans, such courses are insufficient and we need more.

F. The Price of Following One's Heart

The ethical and other issues associated with doing research, as well as the substantial amount of work, made quitting the PhD program my main preoccupation during the first two years. I approached a breaking point, thinking I could not handle the amount and the level of work in the required neuroanatomy course taught by Dr. Larry Swanson. Larry is best known for his discoveries related to the basic plan of neural systems controlling motivated and emotional behavior. He was considered the god of neuroanatomy at UCSD. During the spring quarter, I felt overwhelmed by the amount of detail needed to learn to pass his class. Since I couldn't think of how to leave without disappointing a lot of folks, not the least being my parents who had sacrificed so much, I stuck it out, stayed, and buckled down to study. I found my extra gear and did well in the neuroanatomy class, earning the only 100% Dr. Swanson gave out in his exams. The class made me appreciate the complexity of the tiniest parts of the brain. It also helped me appreciate the vast source of energy I had tapped into during this dark period of doubt. In retrospect, I know this potential energy is always there, although often obscured by a mind obsessed with self-centered and negative thinking.

PETA protestors

Gradually research came to hold a special fascination, making the endeavor worthwhile. That was most true when it led to an insight into the human brain and an understanding no one else in the world had. The expectation of those insights provided the motivation I needed to continue. Unfortunately, working with monkeys resulted in becoming a target of the People for the Ethical Treatment of Animals (PETA). PETA protests were a common occurrence at the university in the 1980s and 1990s. I recall an overcast day at the beginning of the spring quarter. I left my office in the Cognitive Science building and headed to the animal lab, a twelve-minute walk to the Basic Science building which housed it. I carried an umbrella since the cumulus clouds overhead seemed ready to make rain a reality.

As I neared the Basic Science building, I saw a crowd gathered near the entrance. There were many young and old folks shouting and waving signs and placards—a typical PETA protest. The protestors seemed more excited than normal on this occasion. I decided it probably would not be safe to walk in through the front door so headed for the side door of the building. I turned one last time to see the group and read the signs: "STOP

Animal Research"; "No More Animal Experiments"; "Animals Have Rights." Then I saw placards with tombstones and names painted on them. One stopped me on my tracks, for it said, "Vivisectionist: Jaime Pineda, Dead" and underneath "Good Riddance." A cold shiver ran up and down my spine, causing the hairs on the back of my neck to stand up. The shiver turned into fear as my mind somersaulted and tripped on thoughts that the crowd would recognize and descend on me, and make the poster a reality. I ran into the building. From that day on, I experienced chills and anxiety whenever I would see a crowd of two or more people with placards hanging around the entrance to the building. The experience sped up my growing ethical concerns regarding the use of animals in research.

Graduation from UCSD PhD program

Like the spiritual path, the path of science opened up a door, and I walked through it. But in looking back, I realize I walked through more like the lacking-in-confidence adolescent of high school than a confident academic. I completed the PhD from 1982 to 1987, and then spent a two-year postdoctoral stint in Psychiatry with Steve Foote. Because of the unrelenting nature of the work, I had little time for anything else during these seven years. The 1980s became a blur. A lost decade *vis-à-vis* the cultural happenings.

In particular, I missed out on the musical scene to the point I cannot recognize many of the classic eighties' songs. I cannot, for example, identify songs by Prince such as *When Doves Cry* or by Bon Jovi such as *Livin' on a Prayer*. This to the endless chagrin of my friends and contemporaries, but especially my current wife, for whom the eighties', and especially its music, turned into the most important decade of her life.

In cold comfort, I recall the words of another colleague of Steve's, Dr. John Morrison, who said that once one earns the PhD, they cannot take away the achievement. It becomes a source of pride. While I agree, I have subsequently learned that to scale that particular mountain is not the end of academic work. It is but a beginning, for there are many more hills and mountains to climb. A few, such as getting tenure, are even taller and scarier than the PhD hurdle itself. Getting a PhD opened a window into a universe of scientific possibilities, a place where I initially felt comfortable.

CHAPTER FOUR
Challenges of Academia

It's the procession of the lights before the dying sun
That triggers thoughts of fearless fights,
Of rage against the dying light,
As I drive gently into the night.

A. A Unique Academic Opportunity

Having a PhD offers the prospect of getting a faculty job, which can be a daunting task. In my case, it came with the opportunity to join an exciting new academic discipline with a lot of promise in understanding the relationship between mind and brain. This unique chance was godsend, for such events are rare if one considers the history of psychology. As a discipline, psychology traces back to the early Greeks, but did not emerge as a separate field until the late 1800s. To have a new department in the specific area of my interest, to have this new enterprise blossom in the city I lived in, and have it offering tenure track positions in my specialty just when I needed such a job, seems to me to be beyond coincidence. And as providence would have it, this job provided many challenges to my ego. It forced me to confront the underlying reasons for many feelings, and in the process let go of the multiple mythologies I harbored.

In 1987, when I completed the PhD, the job market required one or even two postdoctoral stints of two years each before getting a faculty job. I had completed my first postdoc with Steve Foote in 1989 in the

Psychiatry Department at UCSD. I had interviewed for a second position with Dr. Gary Aston-Jones since the market for a faculty job looked grim. Gary worked at Hahnemann University in Philadelphia and had been a colleague and collaborator of Steve's in Floyd Bloom's lab. I had followed Gary's career and his growing stature in the neuroscience field and was excited about the possibility of working with him. When I visited Gary in Philadelphia, he invited me to stay at his home. I thought that was a smart way to get to know me well and assess whether I could be a good fit for his lab. I especially remember when he offered me anise wine as an after-dinner drink. I had never had anise wine before. We talked longer than what normally occurs in a regular postdoc interview. In the end, Gary offered me the job and I accepted. I looked forward to working with him and quickly began conceptualizing studies we could carry out together.

A few weeks before leaving for Philadelphia, the Department of Cognitive Science at UCSD contacted me. The department had turned three years old and was a relatively new interdisciplinary enterprise in the academic firmament. The Chair of the department, Don Norman, told me they had heard of my pursuit of an academic position and wanted to know whether a tenure-track position in the new department interested me. My immediate reaction was "most definitely yes." This surprised me since I had already committed to a postdoc job with Gary. I suppose my response shouldn't have been surprising, as my goal had been to apply for a tenure-track faculty position in the States. Now the opportunity to stay in San Diego and have minimal disruption to our lives presented itself. I could not turn it down. I called Gary to let him know of the new development and of this new opportunity. He responded graciously and was supportive. He understood that a postdoctoral job cannot trump a tenured faculty position.

I gave the requisite job talk at UCSD regarding the blue place and electrical P300 potential work. The one-hour chat proved stressful. I could not help but be nervous during the presentation, fumbling with my slides while looking at a room full of well-known figures in the field. To be sure, the job talk did not reflect my best performance, but apparently proved good enough. The following week the department offered me the position. I was elated and grateful for how easily that piece of the puzzle had fallen into place. I could only assume Helen Neville, my former mentor and already part of the Cognitive Science faculty, had assisted me once again by making the case for hiring me. I never asked her but felt I didn't need to.

Cognitive Science building at UCSD

Now I would be her colleague and equal—an interesting turn of events. The aphorism "who you know plays a big role in how successful you are" kept going through my head and would ring true throughout my career as a scientist. My background in neuroscience, psychology, and computers made me a good fit. But this represented another set of varied circumstances that came together naturally, as if guided by a greater intelligence.

The Department of Cognitive Science formed in 1986 to understand mind–brain relationships became the epicenter of renewed interest. The forging of a new "cognitive science" discipline required the integration of various perspectives. The assumption that a single perspective, such as understanding the biology of the brain, can lead to an understanding of the brain and mind proved naïve. Integrating biology with multiple points of view, including psychology, computation, and sociology, is a prerequisite. The idea is reminiscent of the fable of the blind men and the elephant. One touch by a blind man to the trunk of the animal provides a distorted view of what the whole animal is. The founders of the cognitive science enterprise wisely brought together researchers, methods, and findings from traditional disciplines, including neuroscience, psychology, computer science, linguistics, philosophy, and anthropology. It proved critical to have faculty with a breadth of interest in integrating across disciplines. In particular, these experts would try to answer the question of what intelligent behavior is when it occurs in humans, animals, or artificial life. I became one of those experts.

UCSD had been at the forefront of this new field since the 1970s when a group of pioneers had created the Institute for Cognitive Science. Then, the University became the first one in the country, if not the world, to form a new department focused entirely on cognitive science. It became the first department to offer the undergraduate Bachelor of Arts and Bachelor of Science degrees as well as graduate PhD degrees in cognitive science. The effort helped establish UCSD as the leader in the field, a position it still maintains after thirty years, although rumblings and doubts of just how successful this was can now be heard.

For me, the opportunity to take part in this remarkable enterprise became providential, for it allowed me to focus on what seemed to be a major driving force in my life—understanding mind and brain and thus myself. The training I received in neuroscience during the PhD program, in psychology from my undergraduate career, and in computers and programming from the air force training came together seamlessly in this new enterprise. Coincidence? I used to think so. But after considering the infinite possibilities that came together at the right time to make this happen, I prefer to attribute it to a larger, wiser, and compassionate intelligence guiding the process.

B. Barriers to Entry

As a new faculty member, I was expected to set up a research lab. I assumed my contribution to the cognitive science enterprise would be to model and study cognition in animals from my neuroscience expertise. I immediately called the lab the Cognitive Neuroscience Laboratory, with a focus on the neural basis of cognition. The Department initially provided me with a three hundred and fifty square foot room to conduct the studies. There was a large acoustic chamber occupying a third of the room and in hindsight the space was totally inadequate. I also received approximately $125,000 in start-up money to buy the computers, hardware, and assorted supplies I needed, as well as to pay personnel to help with the work. To my naïve mind, that amount of money sounded reasonable until I learned that other colleagues were receiving four to five times that amount. The difference depended on the type of equipment they needed to do their jobs. But I now know I could have held out for more funds. It made grant funding an immediate necessity.

In my excitement to memorialize the moment and to own the name of the lab, I had professionally made signs I posted on the two doors to the lab. I did not realize that no other faculty had such extravagant indicators of any scientific work going on behind the gray-looking doors to their labs. To my surprise, however, others quickly followed my lead. Soon many had named their lab and procured signs visibly posted on their doors. Advertising where such research occurred, especially animal work, conflicted with the policy of the university. They preferred not to call attention and thus minimize animal rights conflicts.

Whether I could have an animal lab in which animals were housed within the premises of the department became a dispute with the university from the beginning. I lost the fight and had to accept a secure facility in the middle of campus, away from the department, as the location of my animal work. The excitement of a new beginning wore off quickly. The effort got mired in difficulties almost immediately. Within a few years, these problems forced me to make major changes, including a departure from what I considered the core of my work.

The expense and inconvenience of not having my lab within the department proved too much to overcome. For the university, security was of paramount importance since there had been break-ins into labs to free animals. Death threats to animal researchers doing that work was not uncommon. The break-ins had been successful at other University of California campuses and research animals freed and let go into the wild. To many, including me, that made little sense. I could understand a desire to free captive animals if one thought they were being tortured, which is what the animal rights folks argued. But to let rabbits and mice go free into the wild, sentencing them to death, as these animals were depended on human caretakers, was foolish. Similarly wrong-headed were death threats that succeeded in the cancellation of talks and classes where scientists discussed animal experimentation. My lab's location in a centralized area of the university minimized disruption since greater security could be provided. Having the lab far from the department, however, proved to be a significant inconvenience. It required an inordinate amount of time and travel. This inconvenience forced me to make serious choices.

In 1995–1996, after having worked with animals for nearly five years, I closed the animal lab and switched entirely to human research. That kind of work could be done in the department. This represented a significant shift in my research focus, but my assessment of the pros and cons favored such a move. The human work continued the focus on the same topics I worked on, such as attention, yet I needed to broaden them. Social cognition and disorders associated with social behavior, which had been of peripheral interest until then, began to take center stage.

From the beginning, I kept the squirrel monkeys housed in a large cage rather than isolated in individual cages. This provided them with a more natural environment, including tree branches to climb, larger freedom of movement, and a greater ability to interact and socialize. The social behavior of these fascinating animals captivated my interest but I did not have time to examine it closely.

Squirrel monkeys typically live in small groups of 15–30 individuals per group, with both males and females fully integrated in the group. They do not have a strong dominance hierarchy, as is typical of other similar species. Our particular groups never exceeded six individuals, half of whom were female. Although squirrel monkeys are considered aggressive, I didn't observe this aspect of their natural behavior in the small groups.

Female squirrel monkeys are responsible for almost all infant care. Overall both males and females exhibit complex communication behaviors. These include distinct vocalizations and postural displays. The communication sounds and behavioral displays captured my attention. They convinced me of their innate intelligence, for they seemed to resolve arguments with vocalizations different from those used to warn each other of potential danger. Although such social behavior proved interesting, my focus was on simpler things. I was fixated on capturing brain activity from individual monkeys while they responded to sounds or visual events while sitting in a chair.

The broader interest in social disorders began with classroom readings that involved isolated monkeys separated from their mother as young infants. The results were devastating in terms of the infant's ability to integrate into their social group and ability to interact and socialize with other monkeys. What, I asked, had happened in their brain to cause such problems? Could these disorders be reversed? When I made the move to human research, these types of issues and questions took center stage.

Looking back, the switch to studying cognition in humans, and social cognition in particular, was a temporary setback. It took me away from what I felt was my core area of expertise. And yet, the move seemed preordained or at least inevitable as most of my life now seems, in a good and positive way. For as much as there is a similarity between monkeys and humans, there are still huge gaps in cognition even with our closest cousins, the apes. Thus, there are limits to studying cognition in monkeys as a model of human cognition. Studying cognition in humans is really the best way to understand human cognition. The issue that had prevented me from moving in that direction had been the overwhelming and crushing complexity of the human brain and human behavior. Now I had no choice. I was being guided into it.

C. How to Study Complexity Itself?

There were two entrances to my new Cognitive Neuroscience Laboratory. One door led to a large, open area with desks around the perimeter where staff, students, and visitors sat in their own, individual space. At the same time, there were two large work benches occupying the middle of the room which everyone could use—a kind of shared workspace. The openness of the area, rather than having multiple cubicles, was meant to foster greater interaction among students. I used two of the walls of this large space for hanging posters showing off the work the lab had carried out during the past year.

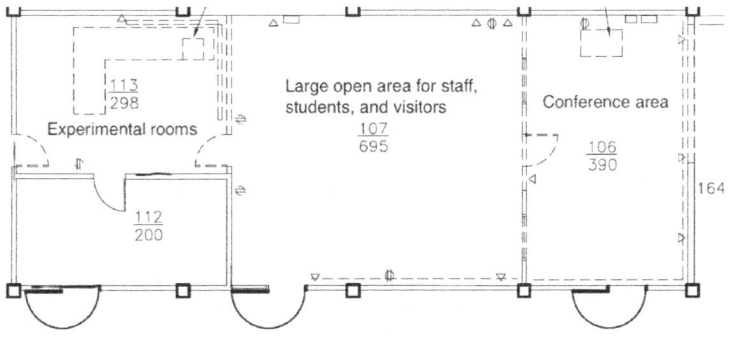

Floor plan of my lab

To one side of this large middle area and separated by a set of glass doors stood a conference area with an oval table capable of holding ten individuals. Here was also the second entrance to the lab. It was in this area where weekly lab meetings typically occurred. I had my desk next to the conference table and would use it as my personal workspace when needed, and as the area where I met students during office hours. On the other side of the lab and separated by a small glass door were two isolated five feet by 10 feet experimental rooms. One room contained the equipment necessary for electrophysiological studies, including multiple laptop computers, monitors, and EEG measuring equipment, while the second room contained a seventy-eight-inch display screen with an eye tracker for visual experiments.

When human subjects were required for our experiments, we turned to the university's well-organized method for online recruiting. This system allowed subjects to choose from among the dozens of experiments taking place at the university, along with the date and time of their participation. Fortunately, the university had a policy of allowing class instructors to require participation in experiments as part of a course or for extra credit. This requirement provided a ready pool of subjects that any experimenter could tap during the quarter. Our experimental sessions did not exceed two hours and so students typically received two hours of credit. We paid subjects around $10–15 per hour to take part if students did not require or need course credit. The system worked well and we had few problems with recruitment of subjects.

My studies recorded brain electrical signals or EEG in human subjects while they performed a variety of tasks involving sounds and visual events, much like in the monkey work. With human subjects we were able to use special helmets fitted with electrodes that subjects could easily put on and take off. Brain signals were then transmitted wirelessly to a recording device.

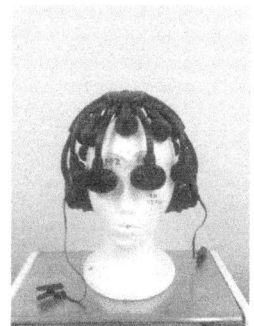

EEG caps

EEG technology for research and clinical work improved considerably in the 1990s and 2000s with electrodes used to record these signals on the scalp, called active electrodes. Active electrodes required no special gels or any other preparation except to make sure it contacted the skin. EEG helmets contained the hardware and software needed to adjust for movement of the head and to minimize electrical artifacts produced by external sources, such as 60-Hz signals from power lines. A subject could walk around the room, or even outside, with the cap on and we could record clean EEG signals. This happened as long as the helmet and recording device, usually a laptop computer, were within a hundred and fifty feet of each other. Instead of recording from only one recording site, we could typically record from twenty to thirty-two channels simultaneously, allowing us to take advantage of quantitative electroencephalographic analysis or QEEG. Using QEEG is a more sophisticated way to analyze human brain signals and obtain visual images of the changes taking place while subjects perform tasks.

My lab also experimented with trying to pattern other animal techniques, like brain stimulation, to the study of humans. Brain stimulation in animal research is a powerful technique because it allows the experimenter to activate specific areas of the brain to see a causal relationship with behavior. Even more interesting, although used with caution and with many safeguards and approvals, is the ability to inhibit or deactivate activity in parts of the brain. I was happy to discover that there were comparable ways to stimulate the brain in human subjects, approved by the FDA and by the local Investigative Review Board.

One technique, called transcranial magnetic stimulation (TMS), involved a way of accurately targeting a brain region with magnetic pulses. A small device is placed on the scalp, oriented toward a specific brain area that can either activate or deactivate a small patch of neuronal tissue. TMS was introduced in 1985 as an alternative to older methods such as electroconvulsive therapy (ECT), and did not have the severe side effects on memory. Thus, TMS became an important research tool in the late 1980s and 1990s. By 2008 the FDA had approved it as an official therapeutic for treatment-resistant depression.

Other techniques, such as functional magnetic resonance imaging, or fMRI, were also available for human studies and included ways to noninvasively image the brain at high resolution while it processed information. In fact, fMRI could not be easily conducted in animals and thus provided a significant new tool in my collection for human studies. This arsenal of tools improved the likelihood of penetrating the impenetrable mystery of the human brain.

By the time I was ready to take advantage of all these amazing tools, I needed larger lab facilities. In a fortunate set of circumstances, I found myself the Chair of the department's Space Committee and hence in charge of allocating space to those needing it. This made getting additional space easier. By this time, Helen Neville had moved to the University of Oregon and vacated her lab space, which I immediately inherited. Like a guardian angel, Helen kept showing up to help me whenever I needed it. Her space totaled thirteen hundred square feet (compared to the three hundred and fifty square feet I had up until then). She had been conducting studies with children, so all the doors in her lab sported a bright pink color. As one walked into the lab, the brightness and force of the color were inescapable. Many people liked it, but many did not. I chose not to repaint and only made slight structural modifications. Like the kids, I found the color soothing, and it seemed to portend my eventual interest in autism and my own studies with young children.

D. The Need for Good Scientific Questions

Vilayanur Ramachandran and Eric Altschuler

Despite the larger lab space and a set of promising tools, I felt lost. For three years during the transition from animal to human studies, I could not get a good research program going. I knew the key was finding a good set of questions that could produce unique and interesting results. Conceiving those queries proved harder to accomplish than I had initially imagined. In 1998, Eric Altschuler, then a postdoctoral student working with Vilayanur Ramachandran in the Department of Psychology, paid me a visit. Eric was smart, blunt, direct, and full of self-confidence.

"Rama and I have been doing work with mirror neurons," I remember him saying as he walked into my lab and got to the point right away.

"What are mirror neurons?" I asked since I had not heard of them before.

"These are cells recently discovered and isolated in monkeys by Giacomo Rizzolatti and his group in Parma, Italy," he responded. "Rizzolatti's group has two papers from '92 and '96 where they report these cells in the frontal cortex of monkeys, in area F5," he shoved the papers in my direction and I began to scan them as he continued. "What's remarkable is these cells respond not only when the monkey executes a motor movement, such as reaching for a peanut, but also when they see others doing the same thing, reaching for a peanut," Eric continued getting excited.

"Do you mean the same cell responds to the doing and the seeing of an action?" I asked incredulously.

"Yes, that's what makes them interesting. It creates an immediate mapping function, converting a doing into a seeing or vice versa," he explained.

"Whoa," I said, "You've got to slow down and explain it more."

"Ok, consider this," he continued while grabbing a pen and paper to show me visually. "Suppose you reach for a pen or paper. We know that cells in motor areas of the brain activate during such movements. Now assume you are watching me reach for the same objects. Turns out the same cells respond. What this means is that watching me reach for the pen or paper creates in your mind a simulation of the movement since you have activated cells producing that action, but can suppress it. What it suggests, and this is the killer idea, is that the reason we understand an action being performed by someone else is because we simulate the same action without carrying it out."

"Wow, that's interesting," I said, trying to fathom the implications.

"We think this is a great discovery, probably even bigger than the discovery of the DNA."

"Now," he continued without giving me a chance to think it through, "Rama and I want to see if there is a way to capture this simulation by measuring the EEG."

"You've lost me," I said.

"It's simple," he proceeded. "Is there an electrical event in the EEG we can record as an index of this simulation process?" "If such an index exists, we can then use it to study it in humans without getting invasive, like we have to do with monkeys." He paused for a moment, allowing me to consider the possibilities. Since both Eric and Rama had MD degrees and clinical interests, I could only imagine they wanted to make a connection to brain disorders.

"Where do we start?" I asked. "Surely you know there is a universe of brain EEG indices. We can't possibly check them all." I had been thinking of the P300 or similar events as starting points when Eric interrupted.

"Here is a better place to start," he said as he handed me another paper. "This paper is by Henri Gastaut and it's from 1952 regarding an EEG brain rhythm they called the "en arceau" rhythm. It has interesting possibilities." He wanted to continue, but I needed to digest all this information.

"Eric," I interrupted him. "You've given me a lot to ponder. I'm positively predisposed to working with you and Rama on this based on what you've told me. Let me read these papers and see what it would take to set up a way to get at this, and I'll get back to you guys soon."

I had agreed to help my colleagues and without knowing propelled my career toward the exploration of this little-known brain electrical oscillation, called the *en arceau* rhythm—or the mu rhythm—as an index of mirror neuron function. It would change the entire focus of my lab. As I learned when reading the papers that Eric had left me, in 1952, Henri Gastaut, a French neurophysiologist, along with colleagues, provided the earliest description of the brain's mu rhythm when they recorded the rhythm in individuals watching a movie. They were interested in how the brain responded to watching movement in the film and when subjects made the movements themselves. The mu rhythm is recorded from the center of the scalp overlying the sensorimotor cortex in the middle of the brain, areas involved in both movement control and sense perception. The sensorimotor cortex contains a motor area mapping the body and controlling body movement, and a sensory area responding to touch, cold, warm, and other sensations. Studies regarding the sensorimotor cortex have come from direct recordings obtained from animals or clinical patients undergoing surgery, and from standard EEG scalp surface tracings made by many researchers. The mu rhythms produced by the sensorimotor area respond to the execution of movement (reaching for a glass of water) and the seeing of movement (seeing someone reach for the glass of water).

We now know this blockade of the rhythm as mu suppression or event-related desynchronization. Gastaut's observations in the 1950s, ignored until forty years later when Rizzolatti and colleagues reported on mirror neurons, made folks like Rama, Eric, and me take an interest in the significance of this relationship.

I could sense from our first meeting with Eric that trying to extract an EEG index of mirror neuron activity had the potential of generating lots of studies and good ideas for research. We were all elated when the approach began to yield interesting results. I grabbed onto this like a life preserver and vest thrown to a drowning man. The idea became the organizing principle behind most of my subsequent work. The positive results gave me a definite boost of confidence. Being in the Department of Cognitive Science, the epicenter of the study of the mind–brain relationship in the world, I now had a solid idea to pursue.

E. Academic Challenges to the Ego

As intellectually stimulating as the faculty job was, it also provided blunt challenges to my ego. My lack of confidence as an academic resulted in trying to validate myself primarily through comparison with others. The list of characteristics and behaviors producing such comparisons ranged from obtaining grants, publishing in first-rate journals, receiving press for discoveries, being invited to symposia, getting students to complete the PhD, receiving teaching awards, etc. When I succeeded and others didn't, I felt good. When others succeeded, and I didn't, I felt wronged and miserable.

This would have been manageable in a small group. But being one of seventeen other faculty members in the department, it meant that a greater likelihood existed for others to be successful instead of me, resulting in more successes on one side of the ledger and a lot of misery on my side. It took me a long time to see the imbecility of thinking this way, but habitual mentation arising at a young age is hard to undo.

The end result was that I quickly convinced myself I did not belong in the company of smarter colleagues who seemed to have it all together. I began to recognize patterns of behavior in which I doubted my own accomplishments. This led to a persistent, internalized fear of being exposed as a fraud. Many career professionals are familiar with this Imposter Syndrome. The syndrome got hold of me early on and would not let go. The internalized fear only grew with time and eventually forced me to face the monster head-on or be overwhelmed by it. The consequence of being in the grip of such fearful thinking is that it robs you of a certain naturalness and creativity, which are so critical for doing good science.

During this time, I was aware of the fear gripping me, an awareness I attributed to my years of meditation and spiritual development. However, it took me additional years before I had the wherewithal to face this monster. When I did, it quickly faded into the background. Surprised and gratified, I realized that my fears were much stronger than the actuality of the thing itself. What allowed me the courage to face this fear? I would say it was the growing understanding of my true nature, the one buried beneath all the mythologies I had created.

This growing confidence reminds me of an experience I had with a postdoctoral student while I was still a graduate student working with Steve Foote and Helen Neville. I had met Dr. Jorge Mancillas at one the Star Trek lab meetings in Floyd Bloom's lab. Jorge had recently received his PhD and worked in Floyd's lab. He was teaching a class I needed to complete my requirements. During a conversation with Jorge about graduate school, careers, and the fear of failing, he casually told me: "You won't believe how much my life has changed since my graduate days a few years ago. I used to be so afraid of things. But one day I decided not be and that has changed everything."

It intrigued me, although literally I could not understand how one could just decide, out of the blue, not to be afraid and have it actually worked. Jorge did not convince or instruct me on how to perform this neat trick, so I did not believe him. It took me an additional dozen years to recognize he was right, and that fear is both an emotion and a cognitive event. Specifically, fear is partly thought and under willful control. I have verified and clarified the truth of this insight in my own spiritual development. Thus, when I finally faced the Imposter Syndrome monster, I had to let go of a deep-rooted thought, but still a thought. And what was the thought that had caused me so much grief? I think it was something that hounded me since grade school, a lack of self-confidence leading to inevitable comparisons with others to justify my feelings.

There were many highly annoying and negative aspects to academia, namely, writing, obtaining grants, and attending faculty meetings. These obscured the many positive aspects of my career. Both positive and negative sides are necessary activities designed to test one's patience and commitment to science. Grants are the lifeblood of research. Without grant money, doing research cannot happen, as there is a need to pay staff and students (both graduate and postdoctoral), and buy equipment, etc. The university does not provide such resources except for occasional small grants for travel or other minor things. Thus, faculty must compete for and gain the money to do their research. Given the competitive nature of the process, the outcome is typically grief and frustration, coupled with anger when a grant is denied, and despair if it happens repeatedly. My aptitude did not extend to being a good grant writer and therefore maintaining a steady source of funding proved difficult. I felt grief-stricken most of the time. While I maintained a steady process of writing grants, both big and small, my luck resembled that with the lottery: rare and without knowing why luck had struck.

Less depressing but equally bothersome was the requirement to attend faculty meetings. As much as I admired my colleagues for their intellect and social proclivities, I could not understand why a fifteen-minute meeting turned into a two-hour marathon and unable to resolve anything. I'm sure others would disagree. Yet for me, faculty meetings were unproductive, with minor exceptions.

Overall, I am proud of my academic life. Despite the challenges, I completed the PhD by maximizing the opportunity, talent, and gifts granted me while positively touching other lives. I enjoyed the prestige of working at a first-rate research university, in a world-class research department, being recognized for the work I did, and having students who wanted to work with me. I find gratification in having survived the expectations and pressures of academia with little resentment and bitterness, having played a significant role in getting students to complete their PhD, and getting many undergraduate students to major in cognitive neuroscience. Finally, I think I contributed to the advancement of scientific knowledge. I can say without shame or regrets that I danced my dance out with all my heart.

Gradually, my dissatisfaction with science came to a head. I was disappointed by its inability to address what I considered real and ultimate questions. What is consciousness? Why are humans so bonded to each other and yet capable of acting so cruelly? What drives our spiritual need? I began to sense limits to what one could know from this perspective.

Research as the Center of My Universe

Are thoughts at rest?
Why don't they tire?
How is pain felt?
What is desire?
When is the mind?
Not in the brain?

A. Observable Conditions

Tim, a ten-year-old boy with high-functioning autism spectrum disorder (ASD) had come as a volunteer to the lab to take part in studies we were conducting. His mom had brought him hoping our work would lead to a breakthrough that would help Tim and others like him. Tim's high-functioning autism meant he could converse and understand instructions. In fact, he seemed bright and talkative—the right candidate for the study.

"Hi, Tim. I'm Dr. Pineda—welcome to the lab," I said as I greeted him and his mom on a cool Monday morning in January.

"Hi, Dr. Pineda. This is my mom. Sorry we're late. We came all the way from Encinitas and couldn't find parking since there are too many people. Is it the beginning of school around here? Is this your lab? What is over there? Can I touch it?" Tim seemed like a typical, curious ten-year-old as he entered and began to explore the lab while talking nonstop.

After he settled down, we completed preliminary paperwork and I explained what we would do. I sat facing Tim at a small desk and began to assess his ability to imitate. "Tim, can you do this?" I asked as I put my right hand close to my chest and made a "V" with my right index and middle finger while holding down the other two fingers with my thumb. I then moved the "V" away from my body towards Tim in a slow motion. "Now you try it," I said.

Tim appeared to be trying to make the "V" but had four of the five fingers of his left hand up, looking more like two Vs, with the thumb down. Even more to my surprise, he moved his hand, which he had extended to make the "V" sign, toward his body.

"Let's try one more time. And please pay attention to what I do," I said with a bit of emphasis on paying attention. I made the same movement. Once again, Tim had the four fingers up of his left hand and moved the hand toward his body. After several exercises, I realized Tim had trouble making the gestures, used his left hand to imitate my right hand, and his right hand to imitate my left hand. I also realized his imitation of movement away or toward his body was the opposite of what I did. I realized that while Tim understood the exercise and tried to make similar gestures, he could not do so accurately. More interestingly, he appeared not able to see the action from my perspective.

To test this further, I sat next to Tim instead of across from him and ran through another set of similar gestures. This time Tim did well. Not only was he able to imitate my left- and right-hand gestures with the appropriate hand, but in fact seemed better able to make the gestures themselves. This suggested the problem did not involve an inability to make the physical movement itself, but a problem when Tim tried to imitate gestures if I sat facing him but not when sitting by his side. I concluded his brain had trouble computing the rotation required to understand the one set of gestures. This, as we now know, is a common problem with children on the autism spectrum. It points to there being a problem in the way the brain computes rotation when we try to imitate a person facing us. The obvious question is: Where in the brain is that happening?

In one sense, my pursuit of how the brain relates to mind, or what makes me who I am, has interested everyone, not only academics, from the beginning of time. The philosophical aspects of these questions get to the heart of who we are. Does the mind arise from a material substance such as the brain, or is the brain part of a larger nonmaterial mind? These are the questions inherent in what I wanted to explore. As a scientist, however, I needed to start by studying simpler behaviors I could operationally define. Defining what one wants to study is key. This means identifying one or more specific, observable event or conditions and independently measuring and testing them. For example, autism is a complex disorder and difficult to study. But one could simplify it by operationally defining it as the inability to compute a third-person perspective into a first-person perspective—the rotation problem Tim exhibited. He could see me sitting facing him (a third-person perspective) but not able to make the right adjustments and computations to see me from his (first-person) perspective. I could argue that one feature of autism is this inability to compute rotation. Once autism is defined in simpler terms, we can test it, as I did by sitting side by side with Tim and noticing he could imitate better. And, if the results had been different, say had he remained unable to imitate, I would have had to come up with another idea of what autism is, that is another hypothesis.

By the turn of the century, in 2000, my Cognitive Neuroscience Laboratory had become the center of my universe. Its focus was the study of questions related to my interests, such as those related to attention, motivation, decision-making, working memory, imitation, face processing, and context-dependent actions. While these were the specific and observable events I could study, I literally wanted to know an awful lot. It all boiled down to the question of social skills or social cognition and how the material substrate of the brain creates the immaterial mind. What, for example, made Tim's brain different from mine? Is this difference characteristic of his autism? And where in the brain is the faulty circuit preventing him from computing third- to first-person perspectives?

During the past ten years of my career, I became interested in perception-action systems and mirroring processes, as my interest in autism gained ground. Perception-action mechanisms are features of the brain relevant to social cognition and thus relevant to autism. Memories of my brother, Javier, and his unusual behavior became an important motivating drive to study this aspect of brain function. Javier's need for order drove him to organize his toys by size. Any changes in this ordering caused him to throw a tantrum. I now know this is a common feature of autism. For such children, there is a need for order in an always-changing and chaotic world. The question is: What brain circuits are relevant for the inability to deal with change?

Since the start of my research career, I have tried to understand the mind–brain relationship, driven primarily by a desire to know myself. How do I come into being? Who am I? And how does the "biological me" create the "psychological me"? In the back of my mind, whether this relationship had any relevance to the "spiritual me" had also germinated. I started my professional research career thinking of spirituality as a distinct interest and something I focused on during my off-hours. Gradually, both science and spirituality began to merge and commingle as I discovered the mystery still present in science and the science present in spirituality.

Research mostly took place at the Cognitive Neuroscience Laboratory where I met and discussed ideas with students and colleagues. Here we had our regular lab meetings to discuss progress, and where, in my small office, I had time to reflect on the results. I only left the lab to teach a class, attend faculty meetings, or eat. This monk-like existence extracted its own costs, namely, no time to do much else. The lifestyle suited my personality and interests. It made me realize that what I had enjoyed the most during my stint as a systems analyst back in Miami-Dade: the thinking through of problems, the brainstorming, offering of solutions, and anticipation of potential problems, I now enjoyed as well. All these reflected what I now did daily with my students and colleagues. In fact, my dream had become a reality.

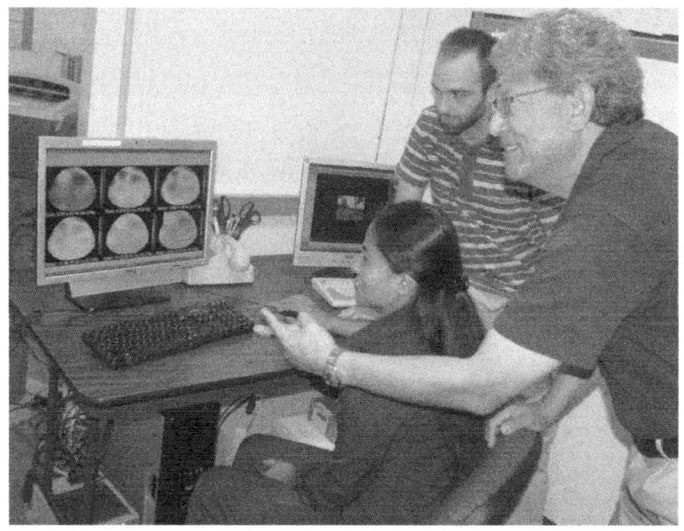

Peering into the mystery of the brain with students

Our understanding concerning mind–brain relationship inevitably changes and so do the questions, as we uncover and unpack the dense foliage hiding its secrets. I decided the best approach I could take in this effort demanded a description of how neural circuits interact and integrate information. There were four general areas I studied. First of all, how the specific translation between mind and brain occurs. This is clear in the example of Tim, the high-functioning autistic child who could not imitate me when facing him but could do so when sitting side by side. What his inability suggested is that Tim would have a difficult time understanding others in a typical social encounter. A lack of understanding of a gesture could lead to Tim's cautiousness in joining a game or in making an improper response. These are typical occurrences for an individual on the spectrum. Thus, my ability to identify the circuits relevant to such a specific problem would help in trying to identify a solution for the problem.

Second, I studied how these translations happen within the context of simple and complex tasks. Tim's imitation of gestures represents a case of dysfunction in a simple task. A more complex task might try to have Tim understand a joke, something requiring greater linguistic understanding. A complex task might require understanding the context of human culture, such as "A Buddhist monk approaches a hotdog stand and says 'make me one with everything.'"

Third, I was interested in how the neural machinery works at different levels of the brain. One level of processing informs and constrains the interpretation of results at different levels, from the single cell level, groups of cells, to networks. I was curious, for example, about what happens in the brainstem when translated into the midbrain, and then to cortex. How does each level inform the others? Can we isolate specific responses to specified events in specific brain regions?

Finally, I wanted to apply what I learned in the lab, the basic research findings, to translational work. Translational work takes basic research and relates it to clinical and practical applications. I determined that Tim and other children with ASD showed abnormal EEG rhythms associated with their inability to imitate or understand actions. I then set out to see if I could correct the abnormal EEG rhythm through basic exercises using a technique called neurofeedback. The basic premise of this neurotherapeutic approach is that the brain is plastic and malleable. Fixing an abnormality by fixing the electrical discharges is possible.

B. Tools of the Trade

I began research as a graduate student using measures of electrical activity, such as single-unit recordings in animals, which are considered invasive. These methods required the introduction of wires into brain tissue of awake, behaving monkeys to isolate activity in a single cell or in a group of cells. Animals had to undergo surgery to make a small opening in the cranium, a craniotomy, to insert the recording wire. To prevent infection when the animal rests between sessions, I sealed and covered the opening, and administered antibiotics. After the animal recovered experiments began. This then required reopening of the window and insertion of recording wires. At the end of the study, the animal was euthanized to determine the location of brain recordings. For a budding Buddhist who wanted to minimize harm to others and do the ethical thing, these approaches became a difficult set of procedures to follow. Eventually, I switched to human research and the method became the recording of the activity of cells recorded on the scalp as the EEG. To do this, I placed helmets containing recording electrodes on human subjects. These electrodes captured brain activity through the scalp and hair and relayed it to a recording device. Because this approach did not cause harm and the helmet could be put on and taken off easily, the research became more in line with my growing ethical concerns. From a research perspective, the assumption was that fluctuations in this electrical signal, or EEG, reflected patterns of information processing in the brain.

While EEG is a measure of electrical activity, the conduction of currents in the axons of cells also produces magnetic signals. I took advantage of this by measuring the magnetoencephalogram (MEG). The MEG looks similar to EEG but is a measure of the changes in the magnetic field. Thus, using both EEG (electric field) and MEG (magnetic field), and other tools, I was able to examine the brain at different levels and from different perspectives. It allowed me a more complete description of mind–brain interactions, particularly in complex behavior.

Jeffrey, a fourteen-year-old young man with short brown hair, had volunteered to be part of our study on brain responses to imitation and face recognition. He joined the neurotypical control group, children who did not have a diagnosis of autism or any other clinical disorder. Like any smart fourteen-year-old, Jeffrey proved curious regarding the study and the facility. He and his dad arrived at the UCSD Department of Radiology in the Sorrento Valley facility to have his MEG recording done.

"It's cold in here," Jeffrey's dad commented as they walked into the room where the MEG machine stood. It resembled a sterile room, with bright lights and a cool 55° with good airflow. After preparing Jeffrey by having him remove all metal objects on his body, I asked him to move into the chamber and to sit on a comfortable chair. I placed the MEG headset on his head and after an initial calibration, the study began.

"You will see images of faces, one at a time on the screen in front of you," I began instructing Jeffrey. "I want you to look at the images and try to keep still and not move."

After fifteen minutes, we moved on to the next part. "Now, a similar set of faces will appear. Only now I want you to imitate the facial expressions you see. Let's do a sample first and then we can begin." After a few images of a happy and a sad face, I asked Jeffrey if he understood the instructions.

"Yes, but do you want me to imitate as soon as I see the image?" he asked.

"Yes," I explained. "Although don't worry if you take a second or two since the expressions are difficult to understand. We present images every five seconds so you have plenty of time to answer."

In both phases of the study, passive observation of faces and active imitation of facial expressions, I recorded the MEG signals from Jeffrey following each event. Afterwards, I analyzed the signals to see differences in his responses to passive and active viewing of different emotions. These were happy, sad, fearful, and joyful faces. I then compared how he, as a neurotypical subject with no obvious cognitive problems, compared to how children with autism reacted.

Across the years, the techniques used in my lab to study mind–brain interactions ranged considerably. They included recording single cells and pharmacological interventions in animals to brain stimulation, imaging, behavioral analysis, and neuropsychological assessments in children with autism. The variety of methods is considerable and neces-sary to bring to bear on complex issues and provide a view from different levels of processing. This progression reflected a growing appreciation of the larger questions of abnormal behavior and led ultimately to the study of disorders beyond autism to schizophrenia and Post Traumatic Stress Disorder (PTSD). With such a progression of interest, I recognized the need for different approaches and the need to bridge animal, human, and patient perspectives. Working with patients added a layer or two of complexity, as the disorder, disease, or injury itself affects brain wiring. "I'm interested in these molecular similarities between autism and schizophrenia," I commented to my colleague, Dr. Fiza Singh. We had both attended a presentation on the molecular basis of autism and were excited to hear the progress being made in identifying genes relevant to autism. "Do you think there are similarities at the behavioral level?" I asked her. Dr. Singh, a newly minted psychiatrist with whom I had consulted regarding our autism work, had her specialty in treating schizophrenia.

Dr. Fiza Singh

"Yes, there are!" she answered excitedly. "I've been thinking the same neurofeedback intervention we're trying with the autistic children could be applied to my adult patient population. Schizophrenia is now considered a disorder of the self and it might be possible to arrest the progression by strengthening circuits involved in social cognition," she continued.

This strengthening of social circuits is what we had been doing successfully with the autism population. We were getting anatomical data showing that the circuits in the brain we were targeting were those being affected, while showing a corresponding positive change in behavior.

"Do you think we would need to target a different part of the brain and maybe use a different EEG rhythm?" I asked.

"It makes sense," she answered, "since schizophrenics have major problems in the frontal cortex and with gamma rhythms."

"Let's talk and see if we can design a pilot study," I responded with equal excitement.

Clinicians like Dr. Singh have as their primary focus helping to resolve the problem and making the patient better. Research scientists who work with patients have as a major focus understanding the mechanisms of the disorder first. The slightly different perspectives can make collaborations between clinicians and researchers difficult. Those who end up collaborating must learn to appreciate both perspectives. This effort is a necessary prerequisite for a comprehensive approach. I found in Dr. Singh a clinician who not only believed in the same methodologies but also had the willingness to apply them to improve her patients. The different interests, perspectives, motivations, and tools made our work unique.

"I think we can start by trying to enhance gamma rhythms over frontal cortex and improve their synchrony between hemispheres since schizophrenics show low levels of gamma and different levels across hemispheres in those regions." This is how Dr. Singh began her presentation a month following our initial conversation. We had agreed to meet to work out the pilot study. She had identified the problem and a solution.

"We can do both things with the equipment and software we just bought," I added. "It allows interactive neurofeedback so a patient can watch a nature video and see and hear the sounds of nature as long as they are doing what we want, increasing gamma and its synchrony across frontal areas. If they don't do that, then the video stops. It's a kind of reward system they control entirely by changing their brain activity and slowly train the brain to produce more gamma and more synchrony," I went on explaining how the system worked.

"That's fantastic," this time another colleague, Dr. Shu, chimed in, "I have patients with PTSD who could use a similar training to learn to control anxiety and stress. Can we use the same program but target a different brain rhythm?"

"Sure," I responded, "but let's not get sidetracked. We can come back to designing a PTSD study next time.

"Sorry, I just got carried away with the possibilities," replied Dr. Shu. Dr. I-Wei Shu, husband of Dr. Singh and a psychiatrist himself, had wide-ranging interests and a specialty in treating PTSD. Both had separate clinics where they treated their patients and both were more than happy to set up pilot studies to address these types of disorders.

Eventually, we set up both types of studies, one for schizophrenia and one for PTSD. The schizophrenia study used gamma rhythms to examine the effects of neurofeedback on memory processing. The PTSD study used alpha and theta rhythms to see whether neurofeedback would affect anxiety and stress. The schizophrenia gamma study proved successful almost immediately and we began collecting significant preliminary data. Once we had sufficient data to show its potential, we applied for a large NIH grant and were successful in getting a five-year grant. The comprehensive nature of our programs fostered creative approaches, driven by both clinical and basic research motivations. It helped to address questions not possible otherwise. Finding such a combination of approaches in a single lab is exceptional. As cognitive science has grown as a discipline during the past ten years, the multifaceted and translational approach I practiced has become the norm.

C. The Best and Most Impactful Findings

One representative example of my research concerns studies in which I assessed brain function by administering legal drugs. Preliminary work had shown me that nicotine directly affects motor responses and working memory processes. Indeed, increases in memory efficiency due to nicotine correlated well with the known functional role of the cholinergic system. This is a system found in all mammalian brains using acetylcholine to perform its function. Nicotine is biochemically similar to acetylcholine and binds to the same receptors producing similar effects. Because acetylcholine helps maintain the state for efficient learning, nicotine likewise produces more efficient learning. These interactions and conclusions are consistent with a model of addiction, arguing that cognitive enhancements induced by smoking motivate individuals to continue smoking and using the drug.

Cigarette smoking is legal and common in the United States I knew that nicotine, the active ingredient in cigarettes, can produce an insidious form of addiction. In a series of studies to study these relationships, I reported that nicotine produces faster reaction times in response to words with emotional content. The public misunderstood these results and I received a strong negative reaction. One example was M.R. from Harrison, New York, age 70, a lifelong nonsmoker. She sent me the following note on November 11, 1996:

> JP:
> MY LOCAL PAPER HAS AN ARTICLE ABOUT YOUR FINDING THAT SMOKING SHARPENS LEARNING, MEMORY & THINKING. Haven't you anything better to do with your time? I consider what you've done to be a plain effort to get publicity for yourself and whoever else worked on the stupid game. There are only two kinds of people who smoke:
> ADDICTS
> IDIOTS

We should do everything possible to rid ourselves of them. With best wishes for the worst.

M.R. contacted me multiple times to express her view and typifies the perspective that smoking is bad regardless of what science might say. For such individuals, ideology trumps truth.

Science is nonideological and aims at getting to the truth. In one of my studies, subjects viewed a list of twenty words called the memory set. Following exposure to the memory set, they were asked to respond to words presented one at a time one way if they thought the word was in the memory set, and another way if it was not. Certain words were part of the initial set (in-set) and others were not (out-of-set). Nicotine administered via a cigarette smoked prior to the test produced faster recognition and responses in both in-set and out-of-set words compared to no nicotine. We call this a "cognitive enhancement" effect. Cognitive enhancement occurred in subjects who smoked just prior to the study and even in smokers who stopped smoking for the twelve hours prior to the study. On the other hand, nonsmokers, individuals who had never smoked, showed no cognitive enhancement.

An improvement in accuracy also accompanied this general facilitation of responsiveness. That is, smokers and those who abstained were more accurate in their responses than nonsmokers. A finer-grain analysis showed that smokers and abstainers responded faster specifically when the target word matched either the first or last items in the memory set. This "primacy-recency" effect is accepted in the human psychological literature as a type of memory we use when trying to remember a list of grocery items. We remember items at the beginning of the list (primacy) and those at the end (recency) more so than those in the middle of the list. Smoking appeared to enhance the primacy-recency effect.

M.R's reaction to these reports were quite negative, as to her they appeared to promote smoking. Logan Jenkins, a staff writer for the North County San Diego Union Tribune, penned a commentary dripping with ironic contempt. He wrote, "Pineda's tobacco findings are just what any doctor wouldn't order: a consoling patch on the arm to the most reviled class of Americans." In other particularly vicious commentaries, I became an unethical shill for tobacco companies. Contrary to these interpretations, my responsibility as a scientist concerned my analysis and reporting of the data we had gathered. I saw it as reporting the truth, regardless of consequences. Unfortunately, these critics did not recognize the practical benefits of nicotine as a memory enhancer—such as using patches to boost memory retention among patients with Alzheimer's.

Smoking changes behavioral performance, which partly reflects how fast we can move our hands and fingers. This can be different than how cognition itself responds. Such a possibility required me to look at the effects of smoking on the brain's electrical responses associated with cognition, namely, the P300, the brain's response to novel and meaningful events. I found that compared with nonsmokers, active smokers produced larger P300s. I attributed the increase in P300 to short-term memory enhancement. Furthermore, I inferred that nicotine, the active agent in a cigarette, likely produced these cognitive effects. However, when smokers abstained for twelve hours and the nicotine had presumably left the system, the differences did not disappear. This suggested that cognitive enhancement occurs from long- not short-term changes to working memory. To me this meant that smokers reorganized their working memory circuitry over the course of their smoking history. And that such reorganization produced the cognitive enhancements.

In retrospect, these research threads produced a significant amount of work, much of which found its way into journals. For the most part, science is a rigorous and direct approach to getting at the truth. Scientists work under a peer review process in which decisions involving relevance and the ability to publish depend on peers. These are other scientists in the same area of research, although not necessarily friends and colleagues. It's a system allowing the best and most impactful findings to find their way into the public sphere. Unfortunately, there are distortions in the system. There are, for example, hundreds of journals, from top-tier to scam publications, allowing authors to shop around until their manuscript gets accepted. A more serious distortion occurs when not everyone acknowledges conflicts of interest, biases, or friendships when assessing the work of others. Even if one doesn't know or collaborate with another researcher, their notoriety might such that personal experience isn't the relevant matter. Since the peer review process applies to grants, the same problems occur there.

I received an invitation to be part of a review committee for the National Institutes of Health to comment on several grants in my area of expertise. It was the beginning of June in 2000, and spring classes were coming to an end. I accepted the invitation, as the university expected me to do as part of my service to the larger science community. On a cold October morning in Washington D.C., I made my way to the hotel where the meeting would be. As usual, there were at least thirty people sitting around a large oval set of tables. We had our names on placards in front so everyone else could read them. I had considered not wearing a suit but thought better of it since Washington is such a formal city. Besides it would keep me warmer. As I looked around and saw every man wearing a suit, I smiled for I had made the right decision.

"Good morning everyone. Thanks for being here. We will start right away, since we have a lot of work to do, and consider the first grant," so said the Chair of the group. He was a familiar name in the cognitive neuroscience field, and we all dove into our reviewer modes. "This grant is from a well-known neuroscientist who has collaborated with many of us, so I will first ask for anyone who has a potential conflict to please leave the room," the Chair continued.

As several individuals got up to leave, I quickly scanned the grant. It did not directly involve me, although I did recognize the name of the principal investigator immediately. A well-known researcher in the autism field. I had not worked with him before and therefore did not have a conflict assessing the grant.

"Let's have the primary reviewer give his assessment," the Chair of the committee instructed.

"Ok, hi I'm Mike Smith, from the University of Pennsylvania and had the pleasure of reviewing this grant from Dr. Grant. As you all know, who are in this field, Dr. Grant is a national treasure for all the excellent work he's done in the past twenty-odd years. His grant continues that trajectory, so let me review what he's proposing."

As Dr. Smith droned on, I caught a few odd sentences inserted in the middle of the description of the proposed studies. It seemed as if Dr. Smith wanted to argue that because of who the person was and the fact he had had continuous funding for twenty years, there was little reason to deny him this grant. The rationale stunned me because of the implication that we should grant funding based on fame and previous work not the quality of the present application. The argument took me by surprise. And as I looked around, I could see from the puzzled expression on other people's faces that the rationale was a problem. It surprised me when we approved the grant.

Given the secret nature of the voting, I could not determine who had given their vote of approval based on the prominence of the researcher or because of the strength of his proposal. Ultimately, despite such potential distortions, science is a sincere and honest effort to get at the truth. And a good career choice. One I would encourage my son to follow. I don't have the angst toward my profession that Dad had toward his.

D. Larger Lessons Learned

From a general scientific point of view, my research did not produce major, earth-shattering discoveries. Instead, my interpretation is that the accumulated evidence gives small insights to help move our knowledge concerning the mind and its relationship to the brain a bit further. The main significance of what I accomplished lies in bringing to bear a multifaceted perspective to an understanding of these complex relationships. My goals required mapping cognitive processes to neural substrates and studying processing at different levels of neural functioning. Understanding cognition and its neural substrates required bridging animal, human, and patient findings to more fully understand them. Finally, developing practical applications grounded in basic research proved to be another approach to help patients, a patient-centered approach leading to observations and results unanticipated in a more circumscribed research enterprise.

From a more personal point of view, did my work of twenty-eight years in science provide insights relevant to this life review? Perhaps the most important one for the understanding of who and what I am is the understanding that one cannot separate mind and brain. Unlike the most commonly accepted metaphor that the brain is a computer running software, representing the mind, in the actual brain, the distinction is difficult to make, for the hardware is the software. Actual physical changes occur in cells as they process stimuli. This produces distinct responses to subsequent input. Therefore, different outcomes occur. Not in the sense that a report is different, but rather in the sense that everything changes, including the timing of when neural events happen, the relationship with the context in which an event occurs, the response to the next event, the physical connections, etc. The brain is "plastic" because its circuitry changes in substantial ways to accommodate the patterns of sensory experiences that wash over it.

Related to this understanding of plasticity is the important idea that the relationship between mind and brain is bidirectional. The brain affects the mind as much as the mind affects the brain. If damage to a part of the brain occurs, such as the hippocampus, it will show up as abnormal memory function. In the same way, when I focus on memory functions and try to improve my memory, new connections and rewiring will take place, resulting in a larger hippocampus circuit. The lesson is that I am what the brain is, and the brain is what I am. But, even more interesting and significant is that the brain and what I am reflect what my environment is. There is a becoming, patterning, reflecting, mirroring occurring between environment, mind, and brain. Because my environment differs slightly from your environment, and my biology differs slightly from your biology, your mind and brain will differ slightly from mine. And my becoming will differ slightly from your becoming, making us both the same, yet different individuals, although still united in commonalities.

In looking back, it is humbling and a source of pride that the field and colleagues recognized my efforts as pioneering and as playing a role in guiding and shaping the cognitive neuroscience effort, even if only by a small measure. As a child from Honduras who emigrated to the United States to get a better education, I achieved a particular dream, and have contributed to understanding an important scientific puzzle while making life a bit better for others. This surprising pathway of science became an opportunity to dance my dance while trying to figure things out.

Science, on the other hand, can fool us into thinking we know. It can trick us into thinking scientific explanations reduce the mystery of life. I can hypothesize, for example, that the physical experience of warmth I feel whenever I read a fascinating book is most likely a reward signal mediated by the neurotransmitter dopamine. This is a more refined guess as to what might go on, but it does not produce a real understanding of the mystery. A scientific approach has provided me with an intellectual and rational bases to understand the unified field of action joining all the different expressions of life. But it is a limited perspective.

CHAPTER SIX

Serving the Science Community

I see the reddish-brown leaves
Carpeting the sidewalk.
I see the intricacy of the veins,
Like some well-planned highway,
And imagine the miracle of photosynthesis,
I realize it is all for my benefit.

Meeting with students in the lab

A. Teaching and Mentoring Undergraduates

It was 2015 and after a long, hot summer, I felt happy to be back in the classroom teaching two of my favorite courses on Mondays, Wednesdays, and Fridays. This particular Monday morning late in September, the new fall quarter started at the university. I was scheduled to teach a required core class for the major on neuroanatomy and physiology. This year, the class already had over two hundred students enrolled and would be the largest class I ever taught up until then. I couldn't be sure how teaching such a large class would affect my teaching style or whether I would need to change my approach. The second class was an elective course on drugs and the brain scheduled for the afternoon. Elective classes held around fifty students. But this one had close to hundred since I had allowed everyone interested in taking it to enroll. I had taught this class for the past ten years at the urging of a graduate student, David Leland, who argued we needed it in the curriculum. He proved to be right, and I enjoyed providing such knowledge to students curious about drugs and drug effects. In between these classes, I would hold two hours of office hours during which I could meet with students who had questions related to classes or other academic issues. I had to also meet individually with my teaching assistants for each of the courses and conduct any other teaching-related business. Thus, Mondays, Wednesdays, and Fridays were my official teaching days, which left Tuesdays and Thursdays to focus on research and everything else, such as attend faculty meetings and other required committee meetings. It was a typical schedule.

Since the beginning of my academic career, I have found teaching to be rewarding. It allowed me the ability to communicate my own scientific excitement but also to bring into the field many new and diverse individuals. Teaching provided a way to give back and share my knowledge with those coming after me. Undergraduates represented an especially important part of my responsibilities. For many of the faculty, teaching is a task done quickly so they can get back to the all-important research. I enjoyed both teaching and research. Teaching involves knowledge. For real teaching to occur, one must know the material well. Practically it means knowing more than students and staying one step ahead of them. Although hesitant at first, I found the daily interactions in class challenging, uplifting, and as opportunities to synthesize and share what I knew. Most satisfying were the discussions of my work, and of the insights and lessons learned.

My teaching philosophy encompassed a bit of mentoring, which is more informal and relational in nature. For one, I felt strongly about educating and training future research scientists in both the classroom and the laboratory. Classroom training emphasized theoretical learning while the lab emphasized practical learning and helping students develop into peers. The combination seemed necessary. That teaching-mentoring perspective oriented me to see lab training as an extended type of classroom and to devote time to preparing for it.

Of similar relevance, I felt training undergraduate students as being equal to training graduate students to the fullest extent possible. When I started faculty life, I encountered an attitude that viewed undergraduates as second-class citizens, of less importance in the research enterprise compared to graduate students. I saw this as a mistake, for I believed that expectations determine the quality of the outcome. Placing high expectations on an individual will usually cause them to excel and rise to the occasion. Lower expectations typically drive individuals in the opposite direction. Thus, the prevalent view quickly became untenable. The seriousness and high quality of the work undergraduate students demonstrated when enrolled in Independent Research classes proved the point. It seemed reasonable to ask: Why can't we use such valuable resources in our own research? Why do we have to depend only on graduate students? What if there are no graduate students to go around? I had confidence that I could train undergraduate students to do the difficult and complex tasks necessary for first-rate research.

I spent a significant amount of time learning how to engage undergraduate students, training them, and providing them with real opportunities to excel in experimental design and in research. My motivation grew out of the treatment I received from my mentors throughout my career. The reward for my efforts was the large number of undergraduates who opted to work in my lab. Hundreds of them over the course of twenty-eight years completed independent research projects and Honor's projects.

Cynthia Mills carried out the first Honor's project I sponsored. I had written a letter of recommendation for her and stated honestly that she, "… demonstrated an unusual native intelligence, a great deal of curiosity, high dedication to the work, patience, wonderful teaching skills, and above all a mature and pleasant personality." When she asked if she could do her Honor's thesis in my lab, I was thrilled. Her work examined the effects of the selective serotonin reuptake inhibitor (SSRI or antidepressant) Sertraline on several distinct memory tasks. The extant literature had not clarified the functional relationship between SSRIs and memory processes. There were inconsistent results. Cynthia hypothesized that this inconsistency arose from the different memory processes being tested. It seemed reasonable to speculate that SSRIs might specifically affect specific types of memories and not others. She and a fellow student conducted a double-blind study in which they gave two different doses of Sertraline and a placebo to normal, neurotypical individuals. Following administration of the drug, they administered a variety of memory tests. The results supported her hypothesis. She found no effects on tests of verbal, spatial, and short-term memory, but significant effects on tests of implicit memory.

Cynthia presented these interesting results at the Annual UCSD Undergraduate Research Conference in 1997. Shortly thereafter she graduated and gained admittance to a graduate program in neuroscience. She earned her PhD in Neuroscience at the University of California, Davis, and is now Associate Professor in the Department of Psychiatry and Behavioral Sciences and the MIND Institute of the University of California. Many others, like Cynthia, came through my lab and had similar success stories. I am joyful in having played a small role in guiding them along at a particular time in their development.

The same principle motivated me to mentor students involved in programs providing research opportunities to undergraduates, such as

The Faculty Mentor, MARC, AMGEN, and Howard Hughes programs. I encouraged all the students I mentored and who worked in my lab to present their work at conferences, typically those organized for undergraduate students. I encouraged particularly outstanding students to follow up with a presentation at a professional conference, such as the Society for Neuroscience and Cognitive Neuroscience Society. Working with all levels of students taught me patience and to see each person as a unique individual, yet the commonality of needs proved noteworthy. Mostly, students wanted an opportunity to be taken seriously, respected, and treated as worthy of trust. In return, they committed all their energy to the effort.

I considered myself a good teacher, a view supported by the relatively good ratings I received from students over the years. I understood the importance of conveying enthusiasm for cognitive neuroscience to those who were just starting out. My enthusiasm for the material engendered the same enthusiasm in the students.

"Hi Dr. Pineda, how are you this morning?" echoed the cheery greeting from Susan, a student in the Drugs class.

"I'm doing great and you?" I replied.

"I wanted to let you know I've changed my major from engineering to cognitive science after your lecture yesterday. I found drug pharmacology so interesting and I felt drawn to it. I can see myself doing research in that area," Susan continued sounding enthusiastic.

"Why don't you come see me during office hours, and we can discuss your doing an Independent Research project in my lab next quarter. It will give you more hands-on experience and maybe help you decide for sure," I replied.

More than anything, many undergraduate students majored in cognitive science with a specialization in neuroscience. I would like to think a main driver of the increase in those majors resulted directly from students taking my classes and becoming fascinated by the subject. In fact, at one point, the number of cognitive science undergraduate students specializing in neuroscience far exceeded other areas of specialization. My Neuroanatomy and Physiology course became a gateway to the major. Whether my style of teaching produced actual learning is up for debate, although little learning can occur if students don't show enthusiasm for the material.

B. Graduate Students

Michael Datko   *Brendan Allison*   *Matthew Schalles*   *David Leland*

The same mentoring approach I cultivated when working with undergraduates guided how I treated graduate and postgraduate students. The main difference between graduate and undergraduate students is that graduate students need little motivation to work on research. For them, research is the reason for entering a graduate program. Grad students are unafraid of hard work and are typically the best of the best. In particular, being available to graduate students as much as possible made up a critical component of my mentoring. The biggest complaint I heard from grad students was how little time their mentors were willing to spend talking and guiding them. In an environment where time is precious because of all the demands from multiple sources, students get shuffled to the end of the priority list. Yet, they have significant needs in terms of academic and personal issues, aside from the research.

I always tried to be available as research and thesis adviser to many graduate students. Doing so renewed my enthusiasm for science and the process of discovery. Several graduates whom I mentored were UCSD and Cognitive Science students, such as Brendan Allison, David Leland,

Matthew Schalles, Mike Datko, Sandra Weber, Adrienne Moore, Emma Marxer-Tobler, and Lindsay Oberman. Others came from local universities and included Kristen La Marca, Sally Miller, Luciano Giromini, Jia-Min Bai, Roy Cox, Max Keuken, and Ron Le Bel.

Brendan Allison was my first graduate student who, through curiosity, intensity, and interests, convinced me to explore a new area of research. He came into the program wanting to study brain–computer interface (BCI) technology and its application in augmenting cognition. In the early 1990s, when he came to my lab, BCI represented a relatively minor but potentially interesting field. Brendan's enthusiasm for this new area of research was unparalleled and contagious. He perceived what few did, that the technology had the potential to help in clinical disorders.

I knew little regarding BCIs, so our relationship started more like equal collaborators instead of mentor–pupil. A BCI is a real-time communication system allowing a human user, who might wear an EEG helmet, for example, to send messages using those EEG signals directly to a device or computer without sending the signals through the brain's normal and natural output pathways. This direct communication allows the human user willful control of a prosthetic device or any other device. Brendan convinced me that by intentionally using electrical brain signals such as the P300 to command and guide mechanical devices, a BCI system becomes possible. In this way I could train a human user to produce larger or smaller P300 signals at will. And with those changes create a metaphorical on/off switch controlling digital devices. For example, a large P300 might signal "I need help" from an immobilized person unable to speak. BCIs allow for closed-loop regulation of behavior using learning called operant conditioning.

I explored the effects of changing brain dynamics on cognition using closed-loop regulation training with a technique called neurofeedback, which is comparable to biofeedback. This procedure uses a BCI providing immediate feedback from a program monitoring and assessing an individual's electrical signals. My work involved using neurofeedback with several special populations, including children on the autism spectrum and patients with schizophrenia and PTSD. Brendan opened up the world of BCI to me and led to what became an important aspect of the translational work I did.

Teaching was always full of surprises. None was more startling than what occurred a few years into my teaching career. In the middle of teaching a graduate seminar on Attention, a familiar face showed up—Francis Crick, best known for characterizing the structure of the DNA molecule and winner of the Nobel Prize with James Watson, walked in and sat down. Francis, then in his eighties, held the post of J.W. Kieckhefer Distinguished Research Professor at the Salk Institute for Biological Studies, just across the street. My initial reaction was that he was lost. I soon realized he actually wanted to sit in on my course. His drive to learn various aspects of brain function characterized Francis's drive for knowledge until the end. My mind went blank. For a long moment I lost my train of thought. But I quickly recovered my composure. Francis came back several times to class, and I survived. Thus, my teaching claim to fame is that I taught this most famous of molecular biologists a bit about attention.

C. Promoting Diversity

My passion for teaching led me to become involved in another major need at the university: promoting a diverse student population. This interest evolved from my first-hand experience in receiving such help and my desire to pay it forward. In 2008, the opportunity to do this in a big way presented itself.

"Hi Dr. Pineda. This is David Artis, Director of the Academic Enrichment Programs," the caller explained while leaving a message in my voicemail. "We are putting together a five-year NIMH grant to support undergraduate students so they get research experience during their junior and senior year," the Director continued. "The goal is to increase the number of under-represented students going on into PhD and combined

PhD/MD programs." Then he got to the reason for the call. "We would like to have you lead the effort and be the Program Director. You have all the experience and attributes for it, and it would increase our chances of getting funding if we could get you on board. Could you think it over and let me know in a few days?" he asked as he signed off.

It didn't take me long to realize what a wonderful opportunity this would mean to help students. I accepted, and the application proved successful. As Program Director for the Minorities Access to Research Careers (MARC) program for five years (renamed Maximizing Access to Research Careers), I helped many students pursue their dream of attending graduate and/or medical school. MARC received a $2.5 million grant from the National Institute of Mental Health (NIMH) to support under-represented undergraduates for at least two years by providing guidance and financial help in their goal to continue their postgraduate education. I placed dozens of students into both PhD and MD/PhD programs over the course of the program.

Besides MARC, I became involved as a faculty mentor and participant in many programs with a similar focus, including the Summer Training Academy for Research in the Sciences (STARS). Students worked in my lab during the summer for eight weeks and got invaluable research experience and advice. The AMGEN Scholars Summer Research Program in Science and Biotechnology resembled the STARS program but targeted students pursuing a career in science or engineering. I had several such students placed in my lab over many summers from The Regents Scholar Research Initiative (RSRI) program and the UCSD Summer Research Program. Finally, there were the Faculty-Mentor Program, Marshall Mentor Program, and APA Summer Science Institute promoting diversity, which I supported.

Hosting foreign students proved to be another way to promote diversity and spread the wealth of the resources available at our university to students from around the world. In particular, I hosted students from

Italy, Germany, the Netherlands, China, and Mexico, as well as students from the American Psychological Association, Hughes Scholars Program, and the Cognitive Science Student Association.

Dr. Amedeo Minichino

One memorable foreign visitor was Dr. Amedeo Minichino, a newly minted psychiatrist from Rome, Italy. Amedeo turned out to be knowledgeable, hardworking, organized, detail-oriented, and a good experimentalist with excellent analytic skills. During his time in San Diego, he worked with me along with Dr. Kristen Cadenhead, in the Department of Psychiatry, on a variety of projects. Dr. Minichino completed an analysis comparing EEG mu rhythm suppression and early psychosis using secondary data we had previously collected. The idea to examine early psychosis originated with him and became prescient. The analysis showed patients with ASD and early psychosis (EP) with active negative symptoms had significant differences in mu suppression in response to biological motion/point-light display animation, compared to healthy subjects. His findings also suggested that similar neural network deficits might exist in patients with ASD and EP with positive symptoms. He published this work in the *Journal of Psychiatric Research*. Dr. Minichino and I also published several other different papers. This was an unparalleled level of productivity for the eighteen months he visited the lab. Following his visit to UCSD, Dr. Minichino applied and entered the DPhil in Biomedical and Clinical Sciences at the University of Oxford.

In sum, the university set the tone for this kind of commitment to diversity so it was not unexpected to get the faculty to take part. I am proud that the level of my participation reflected an above-normal level of commitment, as noted multiple times in my academic reviews.

D. Expanding Teaching Horizons

Teaching, or as I now characterize the venture as "life becoming conscious of itself," provided a rewarding aspect to my academic career. By 2014, I wanted to expand this experience and proposed teaching a summer class in Parma, Italy. Global Seminars are summer courses involving University of California undergraduate students traveling overseas as part of the internationalization of education to take the courses. I proposed teaching a seminar focused on mirror neurons and social cognition and a second one on drug effects in the brain. The Global Seminar allowed me to accompany students to the University of Parma, among the oldest universities in the world. Here we visited Dr. Giacomo Rizzolatti and his group, the discoverers of mirror neurons. By June 2015, I had set the plan in motion and left the States, making my way to Parma with twenty-eight undergraduate students.

Parma is a small town in the northern part of Italy, in the foodie-rich region of Emilia-Romagna known for its Parmigiano-Reggiano cheese and prosciutto factories. The small town has old-style cobblestone streets, a celebrated cathedral, and a baptistry in the center of town. There we were met by Dr. Pier Ferrari, a friend and close colleague of Dr. Rizzolatti, who acted as host and liaison, making our trip a smooth experience. Dr. Rizzolatti, along with Drs. Ferrari and Vittorio Gallese, two additional mirror neuron pioneers, gave lectures in my class. They also set up tours of their laboratories, providing students with a unique first-hand experience of their fascinating work. Being in Parma also gave us all an opportunity to visit different parts of Italy, including Florence, Rome, Pisa, and Cinque Terre.

Vernazza and Liguria

Cinque Terre proved to be a memorable experience because of the natural beauty of the place. The picturesque region is considered the Riviera of northern Italy. It comprises five small villages strung along the coastline making up the region. Along with the surrounding hillsides, Cinque Terra is designated as a UNESCO World Heritage Site. The above pictures are of the towns of Vernazza on the left and Liguria on the right. As I traveled by train from Parma, the terraces built into the rugged and steep landscape right up to the cliffs that abutted the ocean, grabbed my attention. Cinque Terra is a popular tourist area. Once in the villages, the brazen commercialization was all too plain. Fortunately, tourists can only reach the area by boat or train and that has helped to reduce their volume. The magnificence of the area is overwhelming.

The entire Italian experience exceeded my expectations and those of the students. The only downside entailed experiencing the hottest summer in a decade. The Global Seminar provided an opportunity to bond with students, to get to know them as students and individuals, and spend more time together. It was an extraordinary reminder of our common humanity.

During the first visit to Italy, I wrote the following entry in my journal showing that even amid a new and exciting event, my mind constantly wandered into the metaphysics of the experience:

"Thursday, July 23, 2015, one day before my talk at the University of Parma. I have been riding my bike around town for an hour during the hottest part of the day. Sitting on a bench in Parco Ducale, I want to write impressions regarding this Italian experience. On the one hand, the experience would be more enjoyable with Jane, although she could not handle the heat well. All these wonderful experiences last such a brief time, and then the intensity of the experience is gone and a poor replicate left in memory. The present moment is so real, so intense, so precious and yet so fleeting. The mind wants to capture the experience in photos that cannot capture the feelings, nor the 'isness' of the moment. Afterwards, one wonders 'What was real?' Yet the brevity of the experience, while unsatisfying when the experience is pleasant, becomes welcomed relief when the experience is unpleasant. Therein is the beauty of life. Our minds can only experience the smallest of windows of this 'now,' the briefest of the momentary 'isness.' Not sure there is any other way. And yet, the awareness of ourselves as sentient and experiencing beings is continuous. What changes in us are the mental landscapes playing on our mind screen. To focus on the dynamic, never changing mind screen accepting and taking in all our experiences might be more optimal."

On reflection, I find this commentary interesting because I felt I was on the threshold of having a significant understanding of what is real and important in life. I seem to be saying that while our ever-changing experiences are fascinating in themselves, there is, behind these experiences, an unchanging factor that makes the experiences possible. To understand that changeless dimension is worth aiming for.

The rewarding nature of the Global Seminar experience inspired me to repeat it the following year when the weather turned even hotter. My sister, Fatima, and a niece accompanied me on that trip. Sharing the experiences of visiting the Vatican and Rome, the Uffizi Gallery in Florence, and other such places with them made the trip quite enjoyable.

In 2017, I moved the Global Seminar to Sydney, Australia. The rationale for moving hinged on the impending retirement of Dr. Rizzolatti and Dr. Ferrari's move to France. Plus, I wanted to visit a continent I had never visited. By necessity, the focus of the course changed to the evolution of mirror neurons, their development in animals, and Australia's role in all that. My wife, Jane, joined me for the trips in 2017 and 2018. We both found Sydney to be an unexpected and wonderful surprise.

Sydney   *Dinner cruise in Sydney Bay*

I did not think I would enjoy this large city so much. Sydney has the most beautiful harbor of any city I've visited. It is the Emerald City and Land of Oz all in one. Its iconic buildings and places, including the Opera House with its unique shell-based theme, the nearby Harbour Bridge, St. Mary's Cathedral, and Darling Harbour, all add to its sense of dynamism. Definitely a modern city on the move and under constant construction. Add the flocks of lorikeets, white cockatoos, and ever-present Ibis birds around the city and one has the sense of an exotic bird's paradise. Australians are also the most open, untroubled, and friendly people I have met.

Scuba diving at Great Barrier Reef

In 2018 my wife and I made our way to Cairns, in the northern part of Australia. We visited the Great Barrier Reef, a true wonder of the world. It cemented my conclusion that Australia is truly a great place to live. At the Great Barrier Reef, I experienced scuba diving—a combination of snorkeling and scuba diving. Diving into the crystal-clear water of the Coral Sea and seeing the coral reef and multicolored fish all around reminded me of being in an aquarium. It was a fabulous experience, showing me how wondrous the world is, above and below water. The marvel of the reef contrasted with the acknowledged problem climate change is causing. Namely, climate change is slowly killing this sensitive ecosystem as the warming of the ocean produces acidification and destroys the reef. I left Cairns both uplifted and saddened.

Regrettably, the return flight to San Diego produced a minor crisis for my wife and temporarily supplanted my thoughts concerning climate change. She developed pulmonary embolisms from the long flight and required a protracted recovery period. As I write this, my third and last visit to Sydney will take place in August 2019, now as Professor emeritus. These teaching abroad experiences have heightened my spiritual sensibility that students and I are part of a larger oneness. We are the same in terms of our goals, perspectives on life, both positive and negative aspects. What we most eagerly seek is to experience the wonder of the world and of life.

PART III

ENCOUNTERING THE REAL ME

CHAPTER ONE
Developing Crisis

I hear the clarion call,
To something greater than myself.
The mental structures I have built,
That give solidity to my being,
Are slowly crumbling and disappearing.
I see no future.
I see no past.
I don't know how long the present lasts.

A. The "Virtual Me"

Feelings of pride in my academic career did not obscure the fact that my dissatisfaction with science grew proportionally to the development of my spiritual understanding. It's unclear which drove what, and it probably flowed in both directions. The conflicting values imposed by work, included the need to exhibit a judgmental attitude toward others when assessing performance. It also involved continually showing yourself to be better than average by being successful in getting grants or publishing. Finally, it included the ever-present pressure to show and have a scientific impact. All these and more made academic work less than satisfying. The judgmental attitude called for in academia emphasizes the surface value of things and increases separateness rather than valuing inherent being-ness and unity. My dissatisfaction in the value and means of my chosen profession bred doubt and demanded reframing of the question. It called for a new hypothesis regarding what I wanted to do. However, if no answers are clear from one source, one must consider alternative sources. But how did I as a scientist, one committed to scientific facts, become open to the possibility of nonscientific explanations?

The conversion did not occur as a unique "aha!" moment, but as a gradual process. Perhaps the most relevant moments were those in which I began to question the idea that there is a solidity and unimpeachability to scientific facts. I began to realize that much of the core of science requires faith, not a Christian type of faith, but one based on the accumulation of reliable evidence. To take something on faith is not as Steven Pinker has argued in his book *Enlightenment Now*: "to believe it without good reason." That is somewhat simplistic, but unfortunately widely held folk wisdom. Faith is using reason to its fullest extent but recognizing that it is inadequate to the task—that it has limits. If the evidence is unreliable, incomplete, and variable, the assumptions must change. As we learn more, old dogmas fall by the wayside. If not replaced by new dogmas, it leaves us in a state of free fall. Why do we have such confidence that the ground we stand on is solid, when we have already seen this apparent solidity vanish in quantum physics, presumably the most fundamental ground science can stand on? It took me a while to recognize that the ground we stand on for most of science, including cognitive neuroscience, is not as solid as most imagine it to be.

What I see happening in cognitive neuroscience is a refreshing questioning of basic assumptions because we are taking the bigger picture into account. Researchers are no longer satisfied with an understanding of the mind-brain in isolation or only in terms of its neurobiology. We recognize that it is the product of psychosocial, environmental, economic, dietary, and many other factors. The complexity has grown exponentially, and with it the mystery. And yet, there is still a significant amount of blowback toward anyone daring to raise issues beyond the accepted norm, even as the norms are shifting.

As an example, my home Department of Cognitive Science was created specifically to look at mind–brain interactions. But there is at the moment little effort and enthusiasm to study consciousness, the holy grail of cognition. Consciousness in this case, as defined by Wikipedia, are processes "... associated with qualia, subjectivity, the ability to experience or feel, wakefulness, having a sense of self, the claim that there is something that it is like to 'have' or 'be it,' and the executive control system of the mind."

Interest in consciousness drove American psychology from its beginnings in the nineteenth century to the middle of the twentieth century, as reflected in American philosopher, educator, and psychologist George Trumbull Ladd's (1842–1921) definition of psychology: "... the description and explanation of states of consciousness as such." In the early twentieth century, these interests faced doubts about whether the concept of consciousness could in fact explain behavior and whether it is possible to study it experimentally. American psychologist James B. Watson (1878–1958) wrote a paper on "Psychology as the Behaviorist Views It" in 1913, in which he urged that psychology reject consciousness in favor of objective observation and measurement.

The behaviorist perspective of Watson and later B. F. Skinner supported objectivism over mentalism and held sway for nearly forty years. The 1950s introduced a new era of cognitive psychology where researchers discussed consciousness openly, conferences proliferated, and interest reached an all-time high. But, this interest has not breached the walls of the Department of Cognitive Science at UCSD.

Is this a blind spot? Not so much as a conditioned reaction and fear of the history preceding it. Academics tell themselves they know very little concerning consciousness and cannot operationally define it and consequently study it. The consensus in science is that if one cannot operationally define a topic of study, then it is best to stay away from it. And anyone who braves the waters is discouraged, pressured, and demeaned because of those interests.

The impasse we faced seemed obvious to me. I wanted to study consciousness directly, regardless of its definition, as understanding needed to start somewhere. But the pressure to follow any approach considered unscientific proved too great a chance to take while trying to develop an acceptable career. The attitude and subtle pressure forced me to stay within the known and highly studied aspects of cognition.

What is this subtle pressure? I saw it in the rejection of grants for those daring to stray from the main paradigm in the field. It was the promotions that don't come to those considered too daring, the invitations to conferences that go to others more in the mainstream, etc. There is an invisible scarlet letter pinned on those who stray, and everyone in the field knows it.

I recall being at a faculty meeting to discuss applicants to the cognitive science graduate program. My anxiety regarding the lack of students willing to work with me bothered me and so I had widened my search for potential applicants.

"Here is an interesting student, highly regarded, good letters of recommendation and a good letter of intent," exclaimed one faculty in the three-member review committee presenting the findings to the rest of the faculty. My attention perked up. "Everything looks good except she wants to study consciousness and it's not clear there is a fit with anyone in this department. She wants to work with Rama in Psychology."

I wanted to scream. I would work with her and with Rama but could sense the derision and disdain when the word consciousness got mentioned. It wasn't anything overt but subtle looks and smirks at the mention of the word. Part of the responsibility fell on me to make the case for why having such a student would be fine and why studying consciousness needed consideration and encouragement, but I did not have the confidence at that moment to do it.

True mavericks and rebels exist, like my friend and research collaborator V. Ramachandran, or Rama as most people called him. As Professor of Psychology at UCSD, he keeps pushing the envelope. He has done so until the forces arrayed against him give way and there is a new way of seeing things. Then, those who previously criticized now hail the new direction, the new insight, the new paradigm. I recall Rama's comment when he was finally invited to give a presentation in a department seminar that regularly included major figures in the field. Up until then, Rama had not merited inclusion because of his esoteric interests. As he turned to the host organizer, he somewhat sarcastically said, "It's my first invitation to take part in this very distinguished seminar—I guess it helps to have two books published." He alluded to the successful publications of his books, *Phantoms in the Brain* and *The Tell-Tale Brain*. The academic culture could now no longer ignore him.

Much of the assumptions and foundation holding up the science edifice are unseen and unprovable. The best example of this are the basic questions still unanswered: What is matter made of? Why does time seem to flow only in one direction? How did life evolve from nonliving matter? How does a thought arise in the brain? What is the basis for empathy? The list of questions is long. When one knows the tenuousness of the foundation, it is necessary to entertain alternative explanations, even from what I might consider nonscientific perspectives. Traditional scientists are uncomfortable with such an approach.

I realized that the solidity of science, like the solidity of my virtual self (which I will describe soon), is a made-up delusion. This antagonism and tension defined my personal crisis, an antagonism growing to intolerable levels and eventually leading me to come out of the academic closet, to burst out of the straightjacket I felt closing in around me. This became easier to address after receiving tenure in 1996. Soon thereafter, I began giving and being invited to give lectures on esoteric topics, such as Zen and the brain. I would teach entire classes on Zen itself and organize seminars on the limits of science. A slow beginning to be sure, as most of these efforts targeted the undergraduate student population, but a beginning. The various platforms and forums, which occurred during the past five years prior to my retirement gave me a chance to consider and develop the ideas bubbling up inside. When the outlet proved insufficient, I moved outside the academic sphere and retired.

The psychosocial–spiritual separation or individuation I had sensed at three years of age became foundational to my story because a similar, perhaps even the same, sense of separation provided the genesis for my developing personal crisis in adulthood. Ernest Holmes (1887–1960), the founder of the science of mind philosophy and movement, has argued that individuality means self-choice, the unique gift we receive from God. But from the time we receive such a gift, God must wait for us to recognize our relationship to Him. As I grew from childhood, through adolescence, and on to adulthood and began to search for a career, my spiritual search, which I would characterize as my unconscious attempt to recognize God in me, only deepened.

The process of individuation is a slow-developing maturational process that in my case led to the development and separation of what I perceive to be at least two different identities—a real and a virtual me. Awareness of this growing separation fed my personal crisis, eventually leading to a resolution and transformation in my perspective, what I characterize as the realization of my true nature.

I consider the virtual me a psychological creation, a protective mechanism I sensed developing beginning at three years of age. This virtual persona evolved into a safeguard mechanism protecting me from events that might inflict psychological injury. I think of this protective shield as a dense constellation of thoughts, expectations, and perspectives that became a hardened shell surrounding, distorting, and obscuring the real me. The virtual me proved useful at deflecting or minimizing harmful energies, such as the torturous behavior of my sister Nora during childhood, the taunting behavior of bullies during middle school, and the uncertainties of my professional career as an adult. As a professional, the uncertainties included whether I would receive tenure, and if not, where would I move to since I could not remain in the department. It also included the never-ending anxieties concerning grants and not having enough funds to maintain staff and therefore maintain an active research program.

In some individuals, the self-protective virtual mechanism can safeguard them from great harm and horrors, such as mental and physical abuse. Fortunately, I did not experience those things. But, as my capacity for language and for knowing myself and the world grew, this virtual identity became more real—it became a persona. Events occurring around me fostered further reinforcement and solidification of this persona. My sociocultural milieu, the environment I found myself in, all played an important role in reinforcing it. This happened daily.

One morning while getting ready for work, I varied my routine and instead of heading to the Starbucks coffeehouse near my home where they knew me, I went to the one near the university to get my regular, sugar-free, vanilla latte. The coffeehouse is a small, rectangular room with a few tables and chairs at the front. I stood in line, thinking of the class I would be teaching that day. Nothing seemed out of the ordinary, everyone ignoring everyone else, and rather focused on their own thoughts and smartphones.

"What would you like today?" the pretty barista asked me as I made it to the cashier.

I gave her my usual response. "A regular, sugar-free, vanilla latte and a ham and cheese croissant, please."

"We don't have any croissants at the moment," she responded irritated. It surprised me since cashiers are typically very nice and rarely does Starbucks run out of anything. Not having thought of another option, I must have stood there puzzled while contemplating. "If you don't know what you want, please step out of line and let me attend to other customers," I heard the barista say. I could sense her irritation, although I wasn't doing anything other than deciding what else to get.

"Professor Pineda!" I heard a voice say behind me. I turned and saw Susan and Sophia, two students from the class I was about to teach.

"Hi, how are you?" I asked.

"You should try the cinnamon rolls, they're great," replied Susan with a big smile.

When I turned to face the irritated cashier, I saw the same face but a different personality. She had a big smile now.

"You're a professor at UCSD?" she asked somewhat incredulously. "Would you like to try the cinnamon rolls? We'll give it to you for free." I thanked her, paid, and moved on.

The incident that had just happened, a minor and irrelevant one, occurs regularly. Strangers treat me a certain way until they find out I teach at a university. Like the punchline of a joke, their assessment changes completely. I am no longer "nobody" in their eyes, or whatever it is they thought initially. Now they see me differently, as whatever it is they imagine a professor to be. It makes me ask, which is the real me? I suppose I am both a nobody and a somebody, and all the other labels I carry. But who is the real me?

Together, my personality, my history, and the social and cultural environments in which I've lived combined to form what American author Joseph Chilton Pearce (1926–2016) has called the "cosmic egg" or the "mind's drive for logical ordering of its universe." I equate this cosmic egg with what I think of as myself and equate what I think of the real me with this sense of self. But because the virtual me is a creation driven by the need for psychological protection, then the self must be equally created by the need for psychological protection. As I will describe later, the dissolution of the virtual self was, for me, the crack of the cosmic egg that Pearce described.

Both the real and the virtual me are aspects of my developing physical, moral, and spiritual development. The creation of psychological defense mechanisms works well for a time, as it did for me. As I got older and more conscious and sophisticated concerning the emotional and intellectual forces affecting me, this early protective mechanism became less and less necessary. However, because I had reified its existence, meaning that I made it real and identified with it so thoroughly, it did not disappear easily and remains a persistent filter for my thoughts.

When my body and mind reached adulthood, this creation of my untutored mind began to affect me negatively, with a pernicious negativity. It became a nagging voice of pessimism, always present and misdirecting my actions. This virtual persona is at the root of many negative thoughts, but I do not consider it evil, theologically speaking. Rather, it ceased to help me act appropriately to the circumstances and caused me to sometimes act inappropriately. It seems, at least for me, that this virtual persona stopped developing at around twelve to fifteen years of age. And even now in my sixties, when it shows up, I can sense the immaturity, the stunted growth, and prurient teenage thinking it reflects.

How do I deal with it now? I envelop it in compassion for I see it as a selfish, wild, untutored, and undeveloped part of my mind. I tell it things are ok and under control and to not worry. Many times, I simply say, "There you go again" and ignore it. Over time, the inappropriate thoughts have lessened, become less forceful, and receded to the background. They rarely take me by surprise. When they appear, as they will do occasionally, I anticipate them and it gives me time to fortify my understanding and compassionate nature.

In my early twenties, I knew my external persona acted differently from my internal persona. This dissociation helped me understand and unmask the deception. I began to notice how my personality changed depending on which friends and family members surrounded me on any occasion. I became a mild version of a Jekyll and Hyde personality. Or maybe a chameleon personality would be more appropriate. Surrounded by crude and loud voices, I adopted that style, and when around calm and respectful voices, I became calm and respectful. I knew intuitively that such a shifting personality could not be real. I felt strongly that at my core, I had to be the same personality regardless of outside influences. But where was the real me?

At a certain point, awareness of my inner talk became clear, appearing to be the one critical and negative component constantly reinforcing the virtual me. I realized how much I used this inner dialogue to reinforce my thoughts and behaviors. Interestingly, I noticed that the talk took place mainly in the third-person narrator.

"You are such a wimp!" it would say after a particular event I didn't take part in because of my anxiety and shyness. "What are you going to tell your wife now that you forgot your anniversary?" it would taunt me.

The reality dawned on me that this third-person narrator couldn't be the real me, as the real me would address me in the first person. I noticed that such a dialog happened occasionally, especially when I took responsibility for my actions. "I won't lie to her," I would respond to my third-person narrator. Eventually, I assumed this conversation between the first-person and the third-person narrator consisted of an internal dialog between the virtual and the real me. And I began to choose, prefer, and prioritize one over the other.

This insight into the power of self-talk gave me several options. To reframe the negative chatter to a more positive self-talk appeared to be the easiest solution. Yet, such a reframing would only create a different obscuring shell—perhaps a more positive one—but still obscuring the real me. I then recognized that reducing the self-talk itself (mainly from the virtual me) and the possibility of ending this activity presented a preferable solution. I sensed that without such reinforcing energy, there would be a slow dissolution of the shell encasing me since childhood. Would this dissolution reveal the real me? I couldn't tell, as I didn't know who the real me was, and the uncertainty made me anxious. Letting go of this virtual persona and undoing the mythologies of me inscribed in my mind, took on greater importance, for I eagerly wanted to explore this unknown.

B. Dissolving the Mythologies

Awareness of a virtual persona is not common for everyone, for I have met few people, other than perhaps psychologists trained to examine themselves, who have such awareness. Mostly, people stay identified with their created persona all their lives. It usually takes a unique set of circumstances to crack the cosmic egg and dissolve the shell, and with enough of a crack to sense the existence of a more stable and real core.

For me, the set of circumstances resulting in cracking of the egg came from many sources, but primary among them was my inquisitive nature and interest in the question of who I was. For the three-year-old me, the differentiation from siblings activated an unconscious interest. For the older me, science provided a venue in which to ask related questions. My growing interest in spirituality, which provided a potential solution to the "drifting without landmarks" feeling, complemented those efforts. If the sense of self I identified with was a virtual, made-up creation, then its disappearance would invite a frightening emptiness. Who would I be then? This is the conundrum that spirituality and Zen answered for me, because the emptiness I feared is in reality life itself.

Persistent questioning of my true nature led to an insight that *not all was as I imagined*. My mid-life crisis became a spiritual crisis. Fear of being judged as inadequate, as an impostor, made up the thought beneath most of my fears at the height of this crisis. And my most basic instinct became withdrawal, a wish to hide from others, and from life. Once I experienced the initial crack in the virtual me, turning back did not represent an option. For this event exposed a living seed within, which could be allowed to only blossom. It may sound poetic and ethereal, yet in looking back, the reality of it is clear. I did not know initially, but sensed that the virtual me comprised a made-up persona, and that the real me existed beyond this delusion. Once the unreality of the shell became clear, and I engaged in willful dissolution of this delusion, the process became inevitable. My fears lessened, my confidence grew, and the less I wanted to turn away from life. In fact, the opposite instinct—to engage with life—grew stronger. What the virtual me had covered up slowly came into focus.

The existence of the virtual me became a prerequisite for this exposing to occur, as such a mechanism offered psychological protection when I needed it. And we all need it, especially during our early years. However, at some point we also need to let go of this protective safeguard to live life fully. Hence, the cracking event, such as pursuing questions regarding my true nature, is equally necessary for the letting go to occur.

C. Jumpstarting Spiritual Growth

My spiritual crisis, part of a mid-life crisis, dominated my life following my fortieth birthday in 1993. Ironically, my fortieth is the only adult birthday I celebrated in a big way with a big party. It marked a turning point. In 1989, Liz and I had purchased a two-story, three-bedroom house in the Mira Mesa neighborhood of San Diego. When we purchased it, the house stood at the edge of the development in the area. Buying a house had been a major decision. We began to upgrade it with the fervor of the converted. To start, we built a breakfast bar made of tile, without the first bit of experience. We had the motivation, for several weeks, to learn how to cut and lay tile and build a reasonably good breakfast bar. We were so proud of our accomplishment that it led to even greater projects: transforming our two-car garage into livable space and installing cabinets in the dining room. We also had a California room added to the house. All this do-it-yourself activity and house enhancements occurred when Liz and I turned thirty-nine.

The next year, 1993, we invited friends and family to celebrate our fortieth birthdays: mine falling on June 13 and Liz's on July 11. We had converted the garage into an elegant dining area, arrayed with birthday balloons and other such ornaments. My last birthday party had been thirty-one years before. I suppose unconsciously I knew I had reached an important milestone. Unlike a midlife crisis in which getting old, feelings of mortality, and even shortcomings of accomplishment in life become enlarged relative to other problems, my crisis proved to be a crisis of identity. Feelings of depression, remorsefulness, and anxiety were not because I wanted to be younger or wanted a different lifestyle. Rather, I realized the unreality of the self that defined me. And I was overwhelmed with questions. How did the cracking of my psychological shell jumpstart and speed up my spiritual growth? The best answer is that I began to recognize the falsity of the virtual me and sensed that my true personality could be more than what appeared on the surface.

D. Dissatisfaction with Science

Science and the scientific method are humanity's refined inventions and responses to uncertainty. But, just like the psychological limitations inherent in our reactivity to the pain produced by life, there are limitations inherent in scientific exploration—the pain of not-knowing. The solution to both types of reactivities is stillness and an embracing of that which started the reaction. Knowing who one is marks a developmental milestone for all human beings and brings into view the messiness and complexity of life. Mostly, gaining an identity is a self-creation as we attach labels to our biological predispositions and our reactions to the world. We then incorporate the labels others, namely, parents and friends, conceive for us. For most, this is normal and unquestioned, and we play out the created personality until we die. For me, there was a growing suspicion that such creation hid the real Jaime and this led to a growing dissatisfaction.

Adhira, a junior and cognitive science major enrolled in my neuroanatomy class, came to my office hours one day during the winter quarter. She had dark, thick hair, and brown complexion, which I assumed comprised Indian or Pakistani origin. Like most of the students who came during office hours, I assumed she wanted to discuss what she had not understood in the lecture, or to get her score on the quiz from the previous week. It surprised me when, after she had settled down in the chair facing me, she exclaimed, beginning to tear up, "I'm sorry to dump this on you

Dr. Pineda, but I didn't know who else to talk to and you seem like such a nice person."

The compliment pleased me. Still thinking her issue related to my class, I replied, "What can I do for you, Adhira?"

"I don't think I can carry on much longer. I feel depressed and don't see any way out," she continued as she broke down into a soft sob. I wanted to reach out and hug her and tell her things were ok. Whatever the problem she felt, it probably had a solution. But I could sense my professorial persona rising trying to maintain my objectivity and not give in to the emotions of the moment.

"Tell me what's going on," I said, appearing to be calm.

"I don't belong anywhere," she responded. "I don't like the way I look and I don't seem to belong anywhere. My family doesn't care and I don't want to belong anymore."

The implication of her response concerned me, for she appeared to be at a mental breaking point and could conceivably carry out an action she might regret. At the recognition of that possibility, my mental block gave way to a feeling of compassion and love. I no longer remembered my identity, only that she and I were sharing a most intimate experience, and I felt a strong sense of responsibility to help. My cool, dispassionate academic persona gave way to what I would describe as a sense of being part of a larger field with the two of us as instruments in a bigger symphony. It's difficult to describe the feeling and the clearness of my responsibility. I reached out and hugged her, only to make her cry even more and louder. But I could sense a wall was breached, and a space created wherein we could talk. And talk we did. I don't remember how long we talked, for I lost my sense of time. At the end, she and I felt unburdened. While still feeling sad, I knew she would do nothing inappropriate. This real human moment could not have been further from my other academic experiences.

When we see such cracks in our created story and real nature reveals itself, it leads to even more questions. Who am I, if not my thoughts?

Where did this presence, which felt more real, come from? What is the real me? I don't know why such speculations became so important to me. I suppose I could argue my life has been all coincidental, that my natural predisposition to questioning led me to a science career and to the study of the mind-brain, which amplified the questions of my being. The dissatisfaction with answers provided by science then led to searching for spiritual answers. One could argue for such an explanation, although an explanation based on chance and coincidences isn't satisfactory to me any longer. Such an explanation does not ring true, for it is as highly improbable as the existence of life itself. In retrospect, I attribute my life and my interests to the same mysterious force of my youth, which I now see as a living energy, with a purpose, coursing through me and through everything around me. I see the real me as part and parcel of that living energy, which is breaking through, as the virtual me that obscured it disappears.

The scientific path I chose proved to be an honorable, intellectually challenging, and enjoyable one, yet never satisfying. The pursuit produced positive outcomes. However, scientific inquiry is never-ending, and while temporarily rewarding, is never fully sufficient. The complexity of nature is infinite, and each observation produces more questions than answers. I would go down each rabbit hole hoping to understand it conceptually. But, in fact, understanding the entire picture seemed more and more hopeless, for the mystery is impenetrable to the intellect. My Cognitive Science colleagues keep the faith, and many believe we can reach such an intellectual understanding. I see limits in the knowledge science can provide and became less sanguine. Science doesn't make moral or esthetic judgments. It is not self-directed, as it doesn't tell us how to best use scientific knowledge. And it doesn't draw conclusions concerning paranormal explanations.

There is also, inherent in this scientific "objective" or "detached" view of life, a certain abdication of responsibility. From a social and moral perspective, I now feel responsible to not only understand life for the sake of knowledge but also engage knowledge. And to solve problems—or at least avoid creating them. As much as scientists think they can separate themselves from life, they cannot. Many scientists who developed ideas and products that were misused, later regretted having invented them. It is impossible to control the use of anything once we create it, whether an idea or a product. But rather than considering the possibilities prior to their invention, many scientists abdicate such responsibility. From Alfred Nobel and the development of dynamite, to Albert Einstein and the development of atomic weapons, to Kamran Loghman, the discoverer of pepper spray, their future regrets come a little too late. This lack of precognitive responsibility reminds me of the current climate in robotics and the careening of scientists down a path where everything is automatized, with little thought of the consequences. It deeply concerns me that scientists are continuing this myth of separateness and objectivity, rather than embracing the interconnectedness and unity and its inherent consequences and possibilities. As Ernest Holmes wrote "...any scientist who refuses to accept intangible values has no adequate basis for the tangibility of the values which he has already discovered."

There is a fundamental problem created by the current model of research based primarily on reductionism. Because our brains evolved to understand the world by taking things apart, deconstructing the complexity into simpler processes, and processing the individual parts in isolation, the reductionist approach is understandable. It's the easier part. Only a few domains in the scientific world have recognized the more difficult aspect— the integrative one. Cognitive science evolved because of this recognition: that to understand the mind-brain, both reductionist and integrative approaches are necessary. Yet, the problems of integration are daunting and complex. So, while we have devoted a lot of energy to it, we have made little progress. The hopes of artificial intelligence helping to solve the problems of interconnectivity and complexity are premature and, in my mind, unwarranted. The little we know from the scientific enterprise is infinitely smaller than the larger mysteries remaining.

We think we have learned so much. In reality, knowledge rests on shaky ground. What we thought of as established explanations one day, become not quite the right explanations the next. This is science at its best. The question is whether the probing of science ever leads to the truth and not just an approximation of the truth. Toward the end of my career, this question consumed me. Dissatisfaction with science became magnified by what appeared to be limits to intellectualism, and my recognition of the responsibility I had to this larger life. Just like self-talk provided a psychological support system to sustain the virtual me, the academic environment provided a support system to sustain a view that increasingly felt limited and wrong. I concluded that I had to let go of both support systems to explore this new reality. My mind's eye progressively opened to the possibility of a better way of tackling these mysteries coming from the second path my life had taken—the path of spirituality.

In his book *Stepping Out of Self-Deception*, Rodney Smith argues that "spiritual practice is stepping out of the assumed reality of 'me' by understanding what the me is and withdrawing energy from its perceptual fixations." What I came to realize is that spirituality, like science, examines the root of things. I cannot conceptualize these truths only experience them.

CHAPTER TWO
Tragedy and Recovery

Whether life flows
Successfully or not,
Depends on the in-between moments.
It is here that the architects of self-centered thinking live.
Boredom, agitation, expectations, anxiety, doubts, questioning.
In those moments, our untutored mind
Gives free rein to fantasies that hinder the free flow of life.

Family car after the crash. Fatima is in the smaller frame.

A. Answers from Unexpected Places

Life has its way of clarifying problems and providing remedies from unexpected places, from the in-between moments while we wait for answers. I must have received the news of my tenure early in the year, around March 1996. It elated me. Then, three months later, on June 6, 1996, at 6 p.m., a bit of cosmic rebalancing of karma toward the negative occurred. On a rainy mountain road in Honduras, a small red SUV crashed head-on with a large truck. Inside the SUV were my Mom, Dad, and two brothers (Jaimito was 39 and Javier was 30). None wore seat belts. Only Dad survived the impact. But he died in the ambulance on the way to the hospital. While teaching a class, I received the news that something bad had happened and I needed to call home. Whether I learned the news by phone while at work or when I got home, I don't recall, but Liz gave me the sobering news she had received earlier.

What I learned about the accident was that the family had been visiting Nora, my older sister who lived in Tegucigalpa, and were driving back to Comayagua, the town of my birth. Because they may have been drinking a bit, Dad let Jaimito, my younger brother, drive. As they drove up a mountain road, they got stuck behind slower-moving traffic. Apparently, my brother got irritated at the slowness of their progress and thought he could pass the cars ahead. So, he sped up and swerved onto the oncoming lane, only to encounter a large truck barreling down the hill. It gave my brother little time to react on the slick road, and the SUV bore the full brunt of the impact. The truck driver survived and disappeared before the police arrived.

The tragedy rendered my life meaningless for the next few years. Looking back, however, I see a silver cloud. The resulting mental disconnection from all other important matters provided a transitional period for my personal crisis, namely, the dissatisfaction with science and its antagonism with my growing spirituality, to work itself out. Although only after much reshuffling and rethinking of my priorities.

Preparation for and execution of the funeral is a blur. One night following the funeral and while trying to meditate and understand the event, I experienced an unexpected incident. Just before going to bed, I sat mindfully to observe my chattering and grieving mind. It didn't take long before I eased into a state in which a great calmness and quietness pervaded my mind and body. I had no thoughts other than a general feeling of sadness, which quickly dissolved, followed by a river of tears I could not stop. My crying recalled the long-felt absence of parents and brothers, although this time the sensation had no clear emotion attached to it but a palpable finality. I don't know how long the tears flowed. I stayed with the experience.

Afterwards, I felt cleansed and more accepting of what had happened. As devastating as the episode had been, I sensed an inevitableness to it. Not just because of the human errors, the drinking, the impatience, etc., but a more far-reaching explanation. During this moment of meditation, I understood that the four individuals who still lived together—Dad, Mom, Jaimito and Javier—were so intertwined and codependent, they essentially had become one instead of four souls. Invisible umbilical cords connected my two brothers with my parents. Their physical and psychological dependency had only increased as they moved from adolescence to young adulthood. Similarly interconnected and codependent were my parents, now in their seventies and with over forty years of marriage. I felt sure that, because of their interconnectedness, had anyone of them survived the accident, they could not have lasted long without the others.

The recognition of this sense of unity and interdependency eased the pain of their deaths. But then, another recognition struck me. Not only were the four of them connected but so were we all, i.e., my surviving sisters and myself. This "family" energy would continue in existence, although aspects of it were no longer visible to my earthly awareness. This thought was quite comforting.

Tragedies such as this happen unexpectedly and can be both a test and an impetus for spiritual growth. I learned from Liz much later that

Mom had shared a premonition with her. Her passing, she felt, would occur in a freak accident, such as a plane crashing down upon her. It's difficult to describe the mix of sensations and emotions I felt following the car accident, but a recognition of truth accompanied them. The meditation experience was my first vivid encounter with a unified field, an experience greater than myself but one I appeared to belong to. It resonated with and reminded me of the intimate spiritual presence that had always been there for me throughout my life. To view tragedies from this larger perspective does not mean diminishing the sense of loss or confusion they cause. Instead, it simply reminds one there is a larger unity at work, perhaps more difficult to understand, but far wiser than we are.

B. The Mystery of Life

It would be easy to think that encountering a strong spiritual presence would lead to clarification and elimination of all my troubles. But it has become abundantly clear over time that this spiritual presence is Life itself. And, in the flow of life there are always up and downs. The key is how one views these positive and negative events. It would be equally easy to blame the horrific accident for the negative directions my life took going forward. After my meditation experience and the encounter with this Life Force, I have viewed those events from a different perspective and value the direction in which the events pushed me. The accident and its aftermath represented a moment of resolution for me, of gained insights into the mysteries of life. Even with such an insight, I did not realize that the accident had thrown me into a psychological depression. For three years following the accident, any thought of parents or siblings produced the sadness and crying I had experienced during and after the funeral. It was an experience that Joan Didion in her book *The Year of Magical Thinking* has called the "vortex effect." That is, a reaction in which environmental triggers unexpectedly set off emotionally crippling flashbacks. I could as much control the flood of tears triggered by the smallest memory as I could a rainstorm. And yet both tears and rainstorms have a purpose so I did not oppose them. And, like a rain on a parched landscape, it eventually brought new growth. All I can say is that the accident challenged my natural optimism and my understanding of the ultimate goodness of life. It equally challenged my conviction I had all the answers to life's problems.

During the three-and-a-half years following my family's accident, the global community's apprehensions steadily increased with the approach of the Y2K or Year 2000 problem. The basis for the worry concerned software programs that had represented four-digit years with only the final two digits. The year 2000 would become indistinguishable from 1900, which everyone thought would cause serious problems, like the crash of the stock market. Such were the paranoid ideas being discussed. Like individual anxieties, these societal anxieties were equally self-created and eventually proved to be unfounded.

Such unrealized tensions were catastrophically replaced by the real-life devastation that occurred on September 11, 2001. The unexpected terrorist attack shook the foundation of American society. In the months following 9/11/2001, the core of my personal world was also once again shaken to its core. First by the failure of my business start-up venture and then by the divorce Liz initiated in 2003.

After twenty-five years of living together, our marriage had frayed to the point of untenability. My deepening depression surely did not help. But it was more than simple stagnation due to living busy lives with developing careers and being lackadaisical regarding our relationship. From her perspective, my behavior had slowly and inexorably killed whatever love and care we had at the beginning. In retrospect I don't disagree. I was insensitive, callous, inconsiderate, uncaring, self-focused, self-righteous, thinking I had all the answers, thinking I knew more than I did, unable to take her point of view, dismissive of her ideas and insights, especially in philosophical arguments, psychologically immature, incapable of expressing emotion—of saying "I love you"—heavy-handed, did not listen to her advice, and made poor decisions. I had a lot of growing up to do and unfortunately it happened at the expense of our relationship. Whatever bonds held us together had been dissolved by the acid-nature of these behaviors. The relationship could not sustain any new and unexpected stressors. And that is exactly what happened soon after the turn of the century.

I became interested in pursuing business opportunities arising from my academic work. The first opportunity resulted in the formation of a business partnership with a Philosophy grad student named Jordan Hughes. The idea was to buy website addresses for resale. In the early days of the Internet, such speculation seemed possible. Jordan, more of a scam artist than a friend, convinced me of the opportunity his plan offered. Naïve and stupid, I did not seek expert advice. Liz repeatedly tried to warn me of the dangers, but I did not listen. As fate would have it, speculation on internet addresses became outlawed right away, and the business failed.

The money I officially invested in Jordan's company, which he had named Hostcraft, was $160,000. But this was after initially investing close to $40,000 to get the company started. My warped thinking was that I could use the equity in our home to finance this. Because home prices had appreciated considerably, there was a sizeable equity that felt like available money. It did not occur to me that the business would fail. And that I would be held responsible for this "loan" and likely lose the house. I plead guilty to my lack of common-sense.

Liz and I discussed my use of equity money, and she went along willfully with the initial $40,000, but not so willingly when I raised the additional $160,000. In retrospect, she wishes she had not signed the bank papers. She felt manipulated and forced to do so. From my perspective, I knew she felt reluctant but I was not as overwhelmed by the amount of debt being accumulated. Unfortunately, debt kept adding up, especially after Hostcraft declared bankruptcy and Jordan, as CEO, could not pay off the debt. Because I was an officer in the company, I had signed the lease and rental agreements for space and equipment. Hence, I became the responsible party. Again, in my naiveté, I had not anticipated being held financially responsible in the event of failure. The divorce was inevitable. But when Liz filed, I felt stunned.

We completed a "friendly" divorce in 2003, yet the emotional pain remained. The failure of a long-term marriage has mitigated with time and new experiences. Liz and I have remained on good speaking terms, and I have since found solace in a new marriage. Liz remarried as well.

The family accident also considerably affected my research career, resulting primarily in a slowing down of my research output—my productivity. Before the accident, I had set a publication pace of two to four articles per year. This is a rate considered normal to slightly above normal for a researcher in my field in the pace to stay above water in the "publish or perish" environment. Following the accident, the pace slowed down to a single article per year, which is below expectations. The pace began to improve substantially again to four and six articles per year two years following the accident. The slowdown, however, impacted my subsequent reviews and advancement, delaying progress toward achieving full professorship. I could sense the growing unease in my colleagues, and this subtle pressure and expectations complicated things further. Instead of taking six to seven years as is the norm, I needed twelve years to achieve that landmark achievement. I lost five to six years academically. From a personal point of view, I needed those years to fully recover emotionally and intellectually from the searing tragedy. I needed the time for a restructuring of my psyche, of seeing my academic life and its importance from a different angle. It became a time to reconsider priorities and to allow new growth to take hold.

Jane Elizabeth Gilbert

C. Recovery and Remarriage

A year following the divorce with Liz, the negativity rebalanced in a more positive direction. In 2003, I met Jane Elizabeth Gilbert. Jane, born in Minnesota, came to California in her teens. Her family of three brothers and mom moved west in order for her dad, Craig, who suffered from multiple sclerosis (MS), to take advantage of the warmer climate. There were rumors that Jonas Salk had an MS vaccine in the works and they wanted to be near in case of a breakthrough.

Jane and I met through the Great Expectations dating service. Great Expectations, now defunct, required clients to make a video to attract interest. In her video, I saw a lovely girl with a wonderful smile and liked what I saw. "Hi, my name is Jaime. I saw your video at Great Expectations and wondered if you might be interested in meeting for a cup of coffee?" I completed the question without sounding too nervous. I heard the hesitancy at the end of the phone line and thought the effort had been in vain.

"Sure, I can meet you at the La Jolla Pannikin on Saturday at around 2 p.m., if it works for you," the sweet voice on the phone responded and it made me happy.

"Ok," I said, my voice quivering a bit. "I look forward to meeting you."

The La Jolla Pannikin is an old and comfortable coffee shop for locals. And as I learned, an important place where Jane made many of her life decisions. This is where she made the decision to attend law school, to marry the first time, and to have her first and only child. I didn't realize the sacred and important nature of this place. That Saturday started as an overcast, drizzly and winter-like day. Not a good omen, I thought, as I drove the twenty minutes to the coffee shop. All kinds of rumblings were going through my mind. What if she doesn't like me? What if she does? Should I ask her out again? Maybe to dinner? I wonder what she likes to do? On and on… When we met in person, we had an instant connection and I forgot all my anxieties. I only remember wanting to know more about this pretty and interesting woman in front of me.

At the end of our date, Jane casually remarked, "Please call me again if you like." I appreciated her initiative, for it suggested she liked me. I didn't know she had learned this lesson in a dating class she had taken. The instructor had admonished the class: "If you are interested in a person, make sure you let them know." I did not wait long to call her again.

Jane received a law degree from Loyola University in Chicago. The stress, however, led her to decide against actively practicing law. Instead, she pursued insurance claims work in construction defects, which called for the use of her law training. Jane had a son, Victor, from her previous marriage. Fourteen years old when we met, Victor seemed attached to his mother and unhappy at seeing a new male in her life. I remember the first time I entered their condo in Carmel Valley in North County San Diego, part of a beautiful development with small ponds and park-like greenery. The front door led into the small living room. It surprised me to see no furniture and therefore no place to sit.

"We sit on the floor," Jane explained nonchalantly. "Paying for the condo took all my savings and I could not afford furniture," she continued.

"You have a beautiful view from the patio," I said while looking down at the pond where several large koi fish were swimming around.

We sat on the floor and chatted. All this time, Victor sat on the stairs leading to a loft and stared at me. I could sense the resentment, so I tried to engage him in conversation. Unfortunately, he responded with one-word answers and seemed annoyed with the stranger in his home. I felt the same annoyance each time I visited them. Victor's high-strung behavior told me he would need months to accept the fact his mom had entered a new relationship.

As a recent divorcee, I doubted my growing feelings for Jane, and it took me longer to know I had fallen in love. Jane wanted to take the relationship slowly, and I agreed. We dated for two years, giving all of us time to get to know each other better. We got married on March 12, 2005, at the Solana Beach Presbyterian Church. The wedding proved unique in several ways. First, Pastor Dave Gilbert, who was Jane's brother, officiated. Second, Jane's two other brothers, Laird and Roger, came to celebrate the occasion, as did Jane's mom, Ruth, who lived in San Diego. Finally, after the ceremony, we headed to Solana Beach's Beach House restaurant for the wedding reception. The Beach House, on Highway 1, sits literally on the beach. Around 5:30 p.m., we drove west from the church toward the ocean and saw the sun beginning to set. Pale ribbons in pink, orange, and yellow painted the sky in a glorious California sunset. The Earth appeared to be smiling and celebrating with us. The reception turned into a memorable affair. Not just because of the splendid sunset, but because it brought together the most important people to us for a moment of common joy.

A typical California sunset

Jane represented a fresh start, someone without the painful memories of my past. Plus, I felt my previous marriage had forced me to grow as a human being. More than anything, Jane's calm temperament and pure spirit perfectly fitted mine. We knew we would get along splendidly. I could not shake the feeling my mysterious and protective force allowed the opportunity to get marriage right the second time around. The many eerie similarities and connections between Liz, my ex-wife, and Jane punctuated the sense of continuation from my first marriage. Liz's middle name is Mary, while Jane's middle name is Elizabeth. Mary and Elizabeth are biblical names for two cousins who were close. Both Liz and Jane were born in the mid-West: Liz in Wisconsin and Jane in Minnesota. Both had troubled relationships with their mothers. Both have a strong spiritual life and wholesome spirits. I could say I am attracted to a particular type, but the connections seem too improbable to be coincidences. Last but not least, I fell in love with both and both reciprocated those feelings.

Having married Jane in 2005, I faced the choice of returning to my Christian roots. Because her upbringing had been as a Presbyterian, Jane's background represented a slightly different form of the Christian experience, so I felt more than willing to explore it. I began attending the Solana Beach Presbyterian Church, took their introductory class, and joined their small groups. These were groups of parishioners who met weekly to discuss topics raised in the Sunday sermons. What I encountered during those small group sessions were wonderful folks, open to questions regarding God, our own human nature. Above all, they did not feel they had all the answers, but found an equilibrium between the known and unknown. The discussions were deep and probing, and always in a love holding us all in its presence. Had this been all that defined the church, I would have joined and become a member, for their faith seemed genuine and attractive. Unfortunately, what I still heard in the theology, that is, the sermons preached by the pastors, differed from these individual experiences. In the sermons, I heard echoes of my Catholic upbringing: an emphasis on blind faith over honest questioning and an exclusivity regarding the source of wisdom. These intelligent parishioners had found a rationale to make this clear dichotomy work. I could not, since both notions of blind faith and exclusivity in wisdom presented unbreachable barriers for my acceptance of that point of view. I did not become a member, although I still attend church with Jane as a friend and partner.

CHAPTER THREE
Crossing the Gateless Gate

I am confused, unsure, unclear.
The quiet mind has brought me here.
Yet answers are hard to hear.

A. Spirituality as the Naturalness of Life

The tragedy of the accident that killed my parents and brothers, combined with my personal crisis and developing spiritual practice, sped up my recognition of life itself as the living expression of the divine. This life energy has been the protector, guidance counselor, advisor, and direct presence I have sensed from the beginning of my life. What sped up this recognition was my encounter with a way of living that over the past fifteen hundred years has known this reality intimately. Because of the many professional pressures to "publish or perish," my simmering interest in Zen meditation grew considerably in the 1990s to the point of sensing a need to find a teacher. I had been reading and collecting every book on Zen I could find, from classics to obscure ones. Among the ones with the most impact, aside from Watts' *The Way of Zen*, were Herman Hesse's *Siddhartha*, which drew me to the appealing story of Siddhartha, the prince who gave up everything to become the Buddha. Similarly, *Zen in the Art of Archery* by Eugen Herrigel captured my fascination with a unique Eastern way of thinking and how it differed from the mindset I had developed in my childhood and adolescence. Shunryu Suzuki's *Zen Mind, Beginner's Mind* opened my eyes to the possibilities available in the practice's doing. Finally, Rodney Smith's *Stepping Out of Self-Deception* felt like the last book I needed to read to finally understand Zen and the deception of the self. This avalanche of books fed my growing appetite to learn all I could of this fascinating way of being.

What I extracted from these readings is that Zen is a distillation of a way to see and reveal truth. Like science, Zen is fully open to testing one's intuitive experiences and discarding things that make little sense. Puzzling, irreverent, and even mysterious, the ultimate essence distilled, after discarding an awful lot of previously built-up mythologies, is the knowledge that *life is*. But what does that mean? What I have learned after forty years of practice is that life is extraordinary in its ordinariness, and what I have called spirituality is nothing but naturalness interacting with this ordinariness. That *life is* means that each event, each moment of life is special, unique, and perfect—meaning no other possibility exists except the one at that moment. It also suggests that these unique events do not obstruct other events, and all things flow unencumbered to accomplish their functions. This is as close to my understanding of what the Buddhist mean by Emptiness or Great Void, as I can express.

In what most of us think of as normal life, we define miracles to be those extraordinary and special events transcending the moment, which we take as repetitious, boring, and easy to ignore. What I learned to appreciate in Zen is just the opposite. Life's ordinary moments, of talking, walking, sleeping, seeing, eating, thinking are miracles and extraordinary events in themselves. I can vouch as a scientist, and one who studied these topics, that we still do not know how they happen. As we focus, penetrate, and examine each of these ordinary behaviors, we encounter the infinite, the sacredness, the majesty, and the beauty of life. Science and spirituality come together seamlessly at such a time.

Take, for example, the act of seeing, a perfectly normal behavior we perform with so much ease we hardly ever give it a second thought. We typically define seeing as the sensation we experience when light, usually reflecting on an object and within a narrow range of frequency, enters our eyes. Yet, the machinery and mechanics of the eye, let alone of the brain interpreting the visual signals, are extraordinarily complex. We have learned some things, but much remains shrouded in mystery.

And if we recognize the mystery, we let it be. This understanding is more than intellectual understanding, for it does not just make up specific and detailed information regarding the mechanics of the action, rather an appreciation of the aesthetics of how it works. Such an appreciation of the mystery is not superficial, for there must be deep intuition to gain such an aesthetic insight. Unfortunately, I know most of us do not reach such aesthetic insights regarding ordinary things and thus experience a compulsion to ignore or change them, that is, to change the negative for the positive, the bad for the good, etc. Most of my Cognitive Science colleagues, and perhaps most academics, will not understand this because they see life as flawed, problematic, and in need of technical and other kinds of correctives or fixes. What we rarely understand is our confusion of technical answers with real answers, all the while ignoring the deeper underlying truth.

For example, what is behind an inconvenience? Some would argue that inconveniences are the impetus for the technological marvels we have invented. Perhaps. My sense is that ultimately the better solution is not to remove the inconvenience, to find a technical bypass to it, but to address the real issue of why it bothers to begin with. If we examine the real problem, we recognize that what needs to change is our perception of what bothers us. Otherwise we create and give life to a make-believe problem. This begins by examining and understanding who we truly are, getting rid of the egotistical stories we know as ourselves, and seeing the perfect essence we are. Perfect not in a platonic ideal sort of way, but seamless and unadulterated in being the only state possible. And so is everything around. When we recognize this unique reality, our personal energetic flow synchronizes with life's flow. What bothered us previously does not anymore, for the little stream has become the larger stream. I see the inconvenience for what it is. It no longer bothers, and thus does not call for a "solution." We have created technological marvels such as smartphones that put the world's knowledge in our fingertips. Yet these devices are isolating us from each other. I can go down the list. When solutions are devised by a mind not synchronized with life, it can create more problems than solutions.

Reading books on Zen sparked and motivated my interest in this way of living and seeing. What I could not extract from all the reading was a way to actualize and embody the philosophy. This next step appeared to require instructions specific to me and my circumstances. Thus, the recognition came to me around 1994 that I needed a spiritual teacher.

Joko Beck

B. The Need for a Spiritual Teacher

Joko Beck (1917–2011) had become a well-known Zen teacher in the Pacific Beach area of San Diego. When I met her in her seventies, she sported short, gray hair and a grandmotherly demeanor yet a youthful exuberance. I found her to be serious regarding her teaching, yet had a wonderful smile arising occasionally from her seriousness. I liked the fact she had shed many of the cultural trappings of Eastern Zen, including chanting and wearing of the robes. She had developed a new approach to teaching called "ordinary mind." It was Zen simplicity at its finest, which proved tremendously appealing. When I first met Joko, the serenity surrounding her had a striking, palpable, and compelling quality. In retrospect, she reminded me of my childhood friend, Pablo, and the calm aura surrounding him. I began attending Saturday sesshin meditation sessions and then three-day retreats. During each session, I met with Joko in dokusan (teacher–student interviews).

"Zen training," she would remind me each time, "is learning how to work so you do it right, perfect in fact, with no extra anything, whether it is your job, gardening, shopping, whatever. In fact," she would continue, "this requires little sitting—it's more relating to everything in your life and taking care of it."

"Do I need to come to the center to learn to do this?" I would ask.

"Practice occurs anywhere and with anything," she responded. "What happens at the center is I can provide you with encouragement and advice, but the real practice is with your life in every moment. Life becomes your true teacher."

My knowledge of Zen grew slowly as she imparted such wisdom during the four years I stayed as her student. My relationship with Joko turned into an apprenticeship of the heart, one continuing with reading and reading of her book, *Everyday Zen*.

My dissatisfaction with science kept growing alongside an increasing interest and understanding of my spirituality. Eventually, I realized that both paths are opposite sides of the same coin, for they have given me insights into my true nature from two different perspectives. I came up for tenure in 1996. Getting tenure is a landmark event for an academic and being up for consideration stirs many anxieties. I turned to Joko for advice during a dokusan session.

"I feel anxious concerning my upcoming tenure review," I remember saying to the cross-legged Joko.

"Why do you feel anxious?" she asked.

"I guess it's the possibility of failure or not getting tenure that has me worried. I don't know what I will do if it doesn't come through," I responded with a voice sounding higher-pitched than normal.

"Maybe it would be better if you did not get it," she said nonchalantly.

It stunned and confused me. How would it be better? What did she mean? Does she think I have not earned it? My mind began to turn her advice into a self-centered drama. "I have to chew it over," I replied as I made my bow to leave.

"Don't think too much," she commented as I exited the small room.

Her advice floored me and made me resentful of her callousness. Looking back and on reflection, I understand her perspective. I had become attached to achieving such a goal without realizing it. Her advice showed classic Zen understanding. Attachment to ideas and objects is the basis for the discontent and unhappiness that torture a human mind. According to Zen, the best way to deal with becoming attached to ideas is to avoid them. If one can't avoid them, then don't engage them. Don't allow your self-talk to give them solidity. Eventually they drop out of existence. As luck would have it, I received tenure and felt overjoyed. Not particularly a good Zen student, I could not let go of my attachment to receiving such a gift.

Despite not being a good Zen student, I learned several important lessons from Joko. I found the most important lesson to relate to one's teacher. In her view, a teacher is fine to have during the early going, but the best and true teacher is life itself. In this perspective, what is most needed is sensitivity and attentiveness to life lessons. The idea has reverberated in my mind ever since. Little by little, I have turned over my life to this wonderful teacher.

A second important lesson concerned the spiritual search itself. While searching is necessary and recommended, misunderstandings of what the spiritual search is can create problems. For example, the outcome of the search could give a false sense of what is being searched for, as the act of searching itself creates a phantom target. In reality, instead of gaining, the search process is more akin to getting rid of things, like false expectations, ideas, needs, virtual me, etc. Once we have emptied the trunkful of expectations and ideas, we recognize that what we thought missing, and thus searched for incessantly, is in fact already present—a reality uncovered by getting rid of the trappings of the ego. Yet, I needed the continuous and unrelenting practice of meditation to build up muscles of commitment to look where I didn't want to look. I, for one, did not want to look at my attachment to receiving tenure in 1994. Instead, I secretly craved prestige, accolades, and the reward for all my work. Yet, as *Ecclesiastes: 1-12* confirms it, "All is vanity." But it takes courage and committed practice to recognize this. We must confront and uncover the hidden psychological hurts, the expectations we've built up, and face the mythologies we've created head on. When we do, and there are few sticky thoughts or mythologies left, what remains is the nowness of life—the jewel we have been searching for, the naturalness of being. As I wrote in a poem to describe this:

> *Live in the here and now.*
> *For in that space God lives,*
> *And life is real and flows, as it is meant to do.*
> *No problems, no questions, no answers.*
> *Just life being a dancer*
> *Beautifully moving and inter-being,*
> *Creative and all-seeing,*
> *In-and-of-itself.*

Joko further clarified for me what our spiritual search is, namely, recognizing our true nature, the heart of who and what I am, what we all are. What becomes clear and overwhelming when one sees the ordinary, with the naturalness of being, is the recognition that one is part of the whole. There are no discontinuities. One can sense and appreciate the connection with all aspects of life.

This sensibility differed from my scientific mindset, where I saw the world as the object of study and me as the subject studying it. Once I understood that what I am is not distinct from the rest of life, and a sense of unity began to pervade, I could not maintain this scientific duality. In my case, the spiritual insights co-mingled with and pervaded my scientific understanding. When the integration of these two paths occurred, another phase opened up. A phase presumably that is never-ending and has been immensely satisfying because the work here involves clarifying the relationship between my experience of unity and my experience as an individual. We never lose our individuality and the unique ability to see the universe from such a specific viewpoint. Yet, this is only one viewpoint out of many. The totality of those other viewpoints is itself a whole, and you are part of it.

C. Being in Touch

With the family tragedy, my divorce, and a new marriage as backdrops, my inquiry into the mystery of my true nature and relationship to ultimate sources continued unwavering. Gradually, the momentum sped up. Then a change happened. One I would describe as the crossing of a gateless gate, as Buddhists describe it, rather than a big bang. But, in effect, a bit of both. Like my experience as a nine-year-old when circumstances forced me to detach from everything I knew, now I had detached from much of the mythologies of me I had known. And I began to experience moments that slowly reshaped my personality. I would like to think of these changes as more of a realigning rather than a reshaping to what had been there all along. More than anything, I came to appreciate the beauty, sacredness, and nonseparateness from Life. As Lama Surya Das has described, it is an "awakening to the sacred." And, as he describes in his book by the same name, at this point the mystery described in the Tao Te Ching, considered the foundational text for Taoism, becomes understandable:

> *Without going out of my door*
> *I can know all things on earth,*

Without looking out of my window
I can know the ways of heaven.

At a certain point in this period, I stopped automatically killing insects. During my youth in Honduras, while living in our new home in Comayagua, I had become the designated fly killer. In the tropical climate of Central America, flies and insects were inevitable and abundant. I remember the dozens of flies I swatted every day to maintain a fly-free environment inside the house. The goal proved unachievable. Yet I seemed to enjoy the effort, and gave no thought to the flies themselves as I gained proficiency at swatting them, even out of the air. Now, the awareness of their intricate structure, the time to grow such a detailed and beautiful body, and most important their value as predators, parasites, and prey prevent me from killing them. The more the wonders of nature revealed themselves to me, the more sensitive I became. Rather than killing the mice, spiders, flies, insects, worms, silverfish, and other creatures making their way into our home in California, I trap them and release them outdoors. It is with a great deal of pleasure that I now spare their lives.

From this reflexiveness to preserve life, to my growing awareness of the unending textures, shades, colors, and forms of trees, plants, and flowers I encounter in my daily walks, I began to sense the vast intelligence staring me in the face. My nature walks had assumed a spiritual sense as they seemed to bring me closer to the presence I felt all around, besides inspiring my poetic muse. Ultimately, the walks themselves became spiritual exercises.

These feelings were clearly in my mind on an early February morning when I went walking on the beach. The past days were overcast and rainy, not the thunderstorm type of rain but the slow drizzle typical of San Diego. That Saturday morning, the sky cleared. No prediction of rain made my body itch to exercise and walk around. I headed to my favorite spot, the Del Mar beach, and planned to walk back and forth between the Torrey Pines beach area and Dog's beach in Del Mar, a distance of about three miles. I

parked the car three blocks from the beach area in Del Mar and headed
in that direction when a strange thought whooshed across my mind: "The
distance between Heaven and Hell is a change in perspective." I had not
been mulling over anything in particular, and it surprised yet pleased me
by what it implied. "I am in Heaven or at least Paradise," I thought to myself
as the beauty of the day unfolded before me. "But I suppose it would take
one simple thought to turn Heaven into Hell." I continued to muse.

View of the ocean from Del Mar park

By then I had reached the park-like area. As I scanned the horizon,
the majesty of what I saw stunned me. The beauty of life is self-evident,
yet difficult to capture in words. Following the rain on the previous day,
the bright sun had burst through, creating a sparkle in the purple and yellow flowers and in the green leaves of the plants before me. The emerald green grass, just behind them, likewise shone as a layer of moisture
reflected the light. In the background, I could see the white caps of a spar-
kling ocean contrasting against the bluest blue of a sky containing whiffs
of white clouds, looking like adorning pearls. I felt an overwhelming sense

of awe and gratitude at the same time. I stood there gazing and feeling I had strayed into a painting of paradise where every single object stood perfectly. "And I am the beneficiary of all this," I thought.

Immediately, a sense of sadness and guilt flooded my mind. "My God, my God," the thought continued, "Why have you NOT forsaken us? We are the ignorant, the self-righteous, the violent ones, and we do not deserve your grace. Yet, we live with such a blessing, only to forget and not treat it as the gift it is." Tears formed in my eyes as the thought of how humans, who should know better, have mistreated the earthly paradise we have been gifted.

Experiences of such intelligence in nature have accompanied me since youth. As a scientist studying the human mind-brain, I have had first-hand, ringside seat views of this intelligence. The complexity of the mind-brain is profound and infinite, and I do not accept the notion of accidental design. Those thoughts have now become more embedded in my consciousness. The recognition of this awareness is less intellectual and more intimate and personal. I appreciate not just the beauty and complexity of nature but also experience a deep sense of sacredness, gratitude, and an abiding sense of responsibility to do it no harm. I am part of it. Such an inside-out experience differs from my scientific perspective, which is more like an outside-in experience. What I mean is that science brings a third-person perspective to all its studies and insights. We gain understanding from the outside in, a presumably objective knowledge, as if studying life through a microscope.

Spiritual insights give me first-person sensibility, a subjective, inside-out experience. Therefore, I can no longer hold the view that human needs automatically supersede the needs of other animals. Killing might be necessary only if no other options are available, such as for survival, and then one thanks the creatures for their sacrifice. From my new perspective, I cannot conduct the type of animal research I had done earlier in my career. The change of mind comes with a deep sense that vivisection is not right in most of its forms. This new awareness has created a new view of life and of my role in it.

My old self-centered perspective comprised thinking that my reason for living was to adjust and manipulate the environment in any way possible to make it as comfortable for myself and family. Now I see my role as making things as free-flowing and beneficial for others first, including humans, animals, plants, the planet, etc.

Teaching classes primed this new orientation, and the sharing of this other-directed perspective has been a main motivation for this book. Being in touch with life in this way has promoted a relationship between my individual experience and my experience of unity, which I consider a continuous conversation. I don't just "feel" connected to this larger source, I "know" it, like I know the sun will rise every morning. In such continuous dialog, concerns, problems, and mental blockages get processed and resolved almost by themselves. I sense answers in overheard comments, thoughts, a preacher's sermon, TV ads, things I read, etc. It is what I call the dawning of an intimacy with life. Life itself is at work and uses anything and everything happening around me.

In 2016, two friends whom I had known for a while developed cancer, and their entire world turned upside down. As I drove home from work one afternoon thinking dark thoughts, the overwhelming sadness such a disease can bring washed over me. As I approached an intersection close to home, I looked up and saw the red light strikingly vivid against an aqua blue sky. I stopped and stared unthinkingly as whispers of white moisture streaked along the blueness of the California sky.

"What an appropriate metaphor for life this is," the thought entered my mind. "A red light against a blue and hopeful sky." For whatever reason, a calmness pervaded my body, and I relaxed, while the hopefulness of what life can be overwhelmed the thoughts of death. Gratefulness flooded my body.

What I sense in this growing intimacy expresses my true nature. What is happening to me can happen to anyone with an equal sense of caring to know this truth. As the author of *The Gateless Gate*, Mumon has said, "The Great Way has no gate, A thousand roads enter it. When one passes through this gateless gate, he freely walks between heaven and earth." That afternoon at the stoplight, I felt the freedom to walk fearlessly between such a heaven and such a hell.

CHAPTER FOUR
Uncovering the Real Me

I am in the Winter of my Awakening.
The little self has fallen away,
Like leaves on a sycamore tree in Fall.
Winter winds blow through my mind.
Yet there is a presence,
Hinting of Spring,
Of a new becoming.

A. The New Heart-Mind

The year 2012 began with a bang, which then produced an even bigger bang. My promotion to Full Professor materialized in 2012, a full sixteen years after getting tenure, and immediately intensified my psycho-spiritual crisis. From the perspective of my academic career, the promotion felt like the last milestone and the dropping away of the need to reach for more success. The edges of science were closing in. I felt trapped because answers to my ultimate questions, especially those that had accompanied me through much of my life, seemed further and further away. What is consciousness? Why are humans so bonded to each other and yet can act so cruelly? What drives our spiritual need? Why do "I" exist as an individual? Is there a role for me in life? Is what "I" do important? How does my story relate to others? How does it relate to the larger story of life?

In my mind, science was the appropriate venue to get such answers. But the boundaries and sense of entrapment seemed impervious to my intellectual insights. It called for a different penetrating insight. By this time, I was convinced that alternative answers could come from the spiritual domain, although unclear whether one could align the two perspectives. One day while looking for videos on Zen, I came across the Indian philosophy of Advaita Vedanta, or Nondualism, and my eyes were once again opened to spiritual possibilities and to a potential escape from my intellectual confusion. Nondualism looked like natural stepping stones from where Zen had left me, and the bridge I was searching for to connect the various streams of experience. The primary difference between Zen and Nondualism is that the Zen path emphasizes the practice and not so much the end goal. Nondualism, in turn, emphasizes the end goal more than the practice. At this point in my life, I was ready to cross over to the goal itself and thus the appeal of this new philosophy. And, what is that end goal? Nondualism's simple message is: "I am That which I have been seeking all my life."

The essence of a spiritual seeker is the seeking, whether it means seeking God, Buddha, nature, life, your true self, etc. The seeking creates the drive, and the drive creates the "thing" we search for. In this ultimate catch-22 situation intellectual analysis cannot be the key to overcoming the paradox. The key is acceptance of "I am That which I have been seeking all my life." To know I have always been the searched for the "thing" and thus have never lost anything, is both cathartically funny and earth-shatteringly disappointing but overwhelmingly liberating. In my case, it seemed to crash through the boundaries closing in on me. This realization happened directly and *pari passu* with de-identification with the virtual me. Seeing through the imaginary nature of this virtual me, the psychological creation, and the protective cloud developing since I was three years of age, presented me with the recognition of my true self. This reality had been there all along but obscured. Thus, Nondualism presented a more direct route to revealing what I had oriented my whole life toward—uncovering my true nature.

The world did not suddenly disappear nor did choirs of angels appear. One of the most immediate experiences, however, was to see the world differently, as if for the first time, with a sense of wonder about the smallest thing. The dew on the grass in the morning and how beautifully it reflected light drew my attention, as did the intricate details of leaves and colors of flowers and the light on objects. I felt awakened from a black-and-white dream and now the world appeared in technicolor. A hyper-attentiveness, a focused curiosity about the smallest details accompanied this hypersensitivity. But it was not a negative experience, as I imagined a schizophrenic brain that could not filter out irrelevant things and be overwhelmed by the sensory flood. Instead, there was calmness and joy to it, a real delight in the experience.

B. Piercing the Cloud

What made this realization so freeing? How did it affect the boundaries of science that had become so real and challenging? Personally, I felt trapped in a kind of event horizon before this event, with my intellect unable to move forward or backward. I had reached a static state, what felt like the boundary region of a black hole from which no escape is possible—an event horizon. Then, with this new realization, I entered the metaphorical black hole itself, the region in which the laws of causality of space and time change. And with such a step, a recognition of a new beingness. In this new space there were no boundaries, for it is self-evident that boundaries are a creation of the mind's attempt to divide what is in fact a unified field of awareness. I sensed a unity in the world I had not sensed before, and this was enough to free my mind from the feelings of entrapment.

Related to the sense of feeling trapped intellectually, I had also felt trapped spiritually. My relationship to something greater than myself had been a question haunting me for a long time. My growing crisis revealed issues I had forgotten or had set aside as insolvable, including my relationship to Jesus, the presumed son of God, and the only story resonating deeply from my childhood's religious education. I had ingrained Jesus in my consciousness starting in Sunday catechism classes, and now I needed to comprehend his divinity and humanity from my new perspective. The specific question: How does Jesus, another form of the Divine, fit into my new metaphysics? I had a strong intuition that an important transition between my intellect and spirituality included the understanding of this relationship. It seemed critical to my progress. But gaining such an insight had proved difficult. In blunt terms, the question centered on whether I can have a direct relationship with the Ultimate and why I need a middle person or mediator who represents both humanity and divinity. The question is straightforward, but, like a Zen kōan, difficult to penetrate and comprehend. For a long time, this created a barrier I could not overcome. To begin with, the message of Nondualism is not as simple as I have implied. If I am That which I have been seeking, does it mean I am God?

Shankara, born in India around the eighth century and recognized as the founder of the Advaita Vedanta or Nondualism movement, provided one potential answer. According to Shankara, Brahman, the ultimate reality of the universe is the "creative principle which lies realized in the whole world," as Paul Deussen described it. Brahman is the one and only reality, the one existence, the one without a second. The ideas are similar to Western conceptions of God, of a pure consciousness, free from any taint, beginningless, and endless. Shankara argued that Brahman is the only truth, the world is an illusion, and there is ultimately no difference between Brahman and individual self. It is everywhere and inside each living being, and there is a connected spiritual oneness in all existence.

Such an argument makes sense as long as the identity is asymmetrical and one of degree: God has his beingness in me, but I do not have my beingness in Him. I may express divinity, yet to a smaller degree than the Ultimate. It is an asymmetrical identity. But even that explanation does not seem quite right. It became clear that without a mediating relationship, understanding this is difficult. The argument resembles that proposed by

Martin Buber, an Austrian-born philosopher, who considered the distinction between I–Thou and I–It relationship. In his analysis, Buber attempted to understand how human individuality fits into the universality of God. As it relates to my argument, I either understand myself as God or God as myself. Neither of those appear to be entirely correct or fully satisfactory, and thus the need for a third alternative. Jesus, who became the Christ, is a perfect and symbolic representation of an unexplained third type of relationship, or what Buber characterizes as "I am in God and God is in me" relationship. I maintain my individuality as I recognize I am also part of the whole. Jesus as a human being is the embodiment of such an interactivity. Christ consciousness is the actuality that such a possibility is available to all. This insight resonates with me and describes the feeling of my new sensibilities.

This understanding, a dynamic intertwining or inter-being, as Thich Nhat Hanh has so beautifully described, between my individuality and universality, seemed to present itself once the cloud of the virtual me dissipated. To "inter-be" means to see the entire story of creation in every object and event, for everything depends on everything else. Without the initial big bang that created the universe, nothing else is possible. I can say the same for every event following the big bang down to our own appearance. We "inter-are" with all of creation. This sense of inter-being is the real me and the real you.

However, to expect anyone to understand this, who has not been through the same experience of recognizing their virtual self as a constructed reality and then diligently pierce the cloud of such a delusion, is unlikely. The created self, like a crystal lattice, distorts light and therefore distorts the very reality we are in.

C. Contentment to Be

Since 2012, a calm, focused and energized effort to let go of all self-identifications, mythologies, and ideas of who I am, and to know that "I am in God and God is in me" has consumed me. To a large degree, I see the development of these insights as extending the boundary of what I know beyond the intellectual, scientific perspective. Stubborn as I am, I have only experienced a slow letting go of my created persona, a kind of slow-motion unbounding. My individuality is still predominant, but the experience of unity has become more and more tangible. A slow infusion of joy accompanies this gradual letting go and letting be. I used to experience sharp emotional ups and downs. My internal weather could transform rapidly to match external conditions going from sunny (happy) to rainy (sad) to thunder (angry) within a short time. Now, external conditions change, but my internal mood is very stable: sunny (joyful), rainy (joyful), and thunder (joyful).

Several psychological changes have shadowed this gradual emotional development. For one, there is a lessening in my concern regarding time. I can see changes still occurring, such as flowers still blooming in spring, a car speeding down the highway, yet I have a growing sense that the underlying reality of flowers and a speeding car down the highway does not change. A helpful metaphor is the waves constantly forming on the surface of the ocean, which have no effect on the underlying water substrate. Surface reality changes constantly, although the underlying substrate does not.

Letting go of my invented, virtual me has also produced a lessening of the need to search spiritually. For, when the make-believe cloud dissipates, what I encounter is self-evident, and no convincing is necessary. It's like the sun rising and nothing and no one can tell you otherwise. What I encounter is what I searched for and it stares me in the face—it has always been staring me in the face. There is also a lessening in the need to achieve professionally. For it becomes self-evident that our purpose isn't to achieve but to be. If in being there is an achievement, so much the better. As a scientist, I always felt that achievements, such as grants, publications, and promotions, drove science. Now, this feeling is reversed and I see scientific knowledge for the sake of knowledge and its own unique beauty, while associated things are secondary.

Following my realization experience, I have sensed a developing confidence, for I know that it's not a temporary state or another creation of the mind. It is an awakening to an unparalleled interest in life, in what is, unadorned and pure, good and bad. I have slowly developed a sense of the grace and sacredness of all of this. Prayer and meditation have become my engagement and appreciation of this grace and sacredness all around.

These changes do not mean I no longer do life things such as my job or attend a baseball game, or make friends, or make love. Rather, the motivation for doing such things is different. The motivation is no longer to do things to get to a goal but to enjoy the act of doing them. There is an intrinsic joy in being human and able to do routine things. I also sense a paradox in this. A desire to know the unknown motivated my paths in science and spirituality. As I got closer to understanding the true nature of my being, the motivation to know and to do began to diminish. Instead, I found an intense desire to be, to let whatever exists unfold without my interference. Or put another way, to be content without having to do anything to garner such contentment. Since childhood, I have felt an energetic drive providing the motivation to excel and outdo others, to learn, to explore science. This energetic force also facilitated my dissatisfaction, anxieties, discontent, and fears. In my old skin, I felt guilty at not being productive. That energy is still there, but the sense of movement or needing to move is not. I feel calm, yet motivated to learn and explore, and don't experience the anxieties and fears that accompanied my earlier life. I do not feel guilty resting. Instead, I feel energized by not-doing. It is quite an interesting change.

This paradox of being-doing has similarities, at least in my mind, with the paradox of light in which nothing can go faster than the speed of light, estimated at 186,000 miles/second. According to Einstein's theory of relativity, approaching the speed of light makes time run slower and compresses space. Even though an object may travel faster and faster, the speed of light remains fixed at 186,000 miles/second. Presumably, at the speed of light, time and space are no longer valid constructs and reality is everywhere and in every time. Time and space are functions of the speed of light. It might stretch the analogy a bit, but it tells me there are similarities, for I sense that living in the present moment, with a sense of contentment, is to live in no-time. It reminds me of the experience of my childhood when time seemed unending, without concerns, and all I cared about was playing soccer with friends. A more pertinent example is being caught up in watching a movie and losing the sense of time, who you are, and feeling embedded in the movie itself. Imagine if you saw life as the movie you were watching and interested in.

I have also associated the contentment to be with an outward focus and an intense desire to help others. Put another way, de-identification with the virtual me has led to a default in orientation that is more outward-looking. From a Buddhist perspective, the process seems to be a slow waking-up period and the opening of my heart. Or, as the Dalai Lama once said, opening of the heart is more than an emotion. The action means complete commitment to others.

Another change produced by this realization is a renewed creativity, intensity, and focus on free-verse poetry, focused on helping and guiding others on a similar path. Academic work only partially sustained my need for creativity and originality. This new poetic energy began stirring two years prior to my retirement in 2018 but burst forth after the letting go of academic responsibilities. It has already led to the self-publication of my first *Book of Verse: The Quieting of a Mind*. More recently I have completed the second one, *The Dawning of a New Mind*. These are poems in free verse concerning the piercing of the cloud and the encountering of the real me. Over the course of the past three years, my poetry has focused on recognizing the waking-up process and learning to live lovingly and compassionately with awareness.

When I wrote my second book of poems, I recognized that the creativity, motivation, interest, and love for poetry did not exhaust itself by the completion of the first *Book of Verse: The Quieting of a Mind*. As true of my first effort, writing poetry has allowed me to look around, observe the world in intimate detail, and try to describe and express what is profound, exquisite, and indescribable. To enter such a state has, over many years, sculpted my mind and contributed to its quieting. This quieting has intensified my love for life, for being, nature, and those around me. Now I see a new mind, a new awareness growing out of that quieting, and an intensification of life, what I call a new heart—mind. The appearance of this new heart—mind validated my decision to retire from academia after twenty-eight years of being a scientist and focus on these unfolding forces.

D. New, Fresh, and Natural

As I have tried to describe it, this new heart—mind, which came into being following the realization of my true nature, is a new, fresh, and natural outlook. It has an intrinsic joy in being, with a deep and uncompromising dedication to what is true and real. For one, I have less incentive to create untruths, to lie, as I see them as distortions of reality. I often catch myself distorting the truth, especially with what we call "white" or "social" lies, but the incentive of this new mind is to reduce them to a bare minimum.

This new mind exudes grace, love, and empathy toward plants, animals, humans, and the planet. It's the environmentalism or caring for others that springs from the experience or glimpse of unity that makes it clear there is an interconnectedness to life. Take any object, say a chair, and think about what went into making the chair, the individuals involved, the parents who gave them birth, the tree or trees it came from, the nutrients and rain that fed those trees, the weather patterns necessary to create the climate that allowed the trees to grow, etc., and you sense the connections and the interdependency.

The heart—mind does no harm, desires to help others, exudes no competitiveness, and experiences joy in the good fortune of others. This has been one of the most surprising changes I've experienced. From living a life that was primarily self-centered, I have developed a strong desire to move away from that toward a life focused on helping others, as I will describe.

The new mind has enhanced appreciation for pleasure, beauty, rest, life, the present moment. I focus on life as it is, unvarnished and real. I not only appreciate life but also feel a great deal of gratitude for the opportunity to experience it. The new mind has no desire to stand out, to get objects, to do the expected, while it shows little fear. As I've alluded to before, fear diminishes with the growing confidence in life, its integrity, its unity, and deep knowingness of what is right. The heart—mind has an approach as opposed to an avoidance impulse and shows an eagerness to experience the world and human psychological reactions.

One interesting and specific experience I have that reflects this new heart—mind is on sunny days, when light from the sun appears to penetrate the objects I see and create a kind of translucent experience in which the objects themselves appear to be the source of this light. It reminds me of my experience when I first saw paintings by Rembrandt at a Frankfurt art gallery. And how he captured the experience of the inner or divine light so well. At moments, the world seems like a Rembrandt painting, with me in the middle of it and enjoying it all.

In particular, this new heart—mind has a spaciousness unconfined by my brain. Such unconfined spaciousness is a difficult concept to convey because the awareness of it originates outside of my body and includes me and many other aspects of what it is. It contains me. This larger awareness contains all and sees no difference between the tree outside the window, the clouds and blue sky, the bird flying by, me sitting on a chair, the sound of the wind, or the neighbor saying hello. This extrasomatic experience differs from the normal experience of awareness originating inside my body and that I contain what I see and experience. This movement of consciousness from a somatic to an extrasomatic perspective seems to occur more and more frequently and even volitionally.

As someone familiar with Buddhist teachings, what I describe as my realization is consistent with the fulfillment of what the Buddha taught as the Eightfold Path. That is, realization is having the view that life is a unity and that you are an indivisible part of that unity. It is having unbending faith in such a system and confidence that it has good intentions. It is orienting life toward helping others and avoiding doing harm. It is having a continuous practice of maintaining a steady, curious, and inquisitive mind that is both focused and vigilant. It is having an attitude of speech and actions arising from kindness and compassion.

CHAPTER FIVE

What Then is Left to Do?

What is left is to do this dance called Life.
For each dance with the Ultimate is unique,
The point is to enjoy the moment.
For in the dynamics and beauty of it all,
Anything is possible.

A. Helping Others

With any rebirth, especially what may be a spiritual one, there are always growing pains. How can I reconcile my old experience with this new experience? How does this new perspective affect what I think concerning mind-brain? How do I live an ethical and meaningful life when the basis of what has been meaningful crumbles as a fiction that I have created? The only reasonable conclusion I have come to in dealing with all these questions is to trust this larger and developing awareness and let this intelligence be the guide and in control.

On August 4, 2017, while in Sydney, Australia, and a day before heading home from teaching the Global Seminar, I pondered my future. Sitting on a bench at the park by the war memorial downtown around 11 a.m., I wrote:

"It is a beautiful sunny day with a cool wind after the rainfall last night. My thoughts are of my next stage in life. My intent to retire next year is still the plan. I will work this fall quarter and then take a two-quarter-sabbatical. If I need to teach the following fall, I will. Once retirement completes, I'm unsure just how I will spend my time. I plan to devote part of each day to meditation on reality and the '*Who I am question*'—trying to recognize dreams from reality. I envision walks along the beach and other places and being inspired to write poetry. I will look for a community of like-minded individuals. For the other part of the time, my intention is to do volunteer work and continue academic work. I want to teach classes, work as a journal editor, continue collaborations with colleagues, and write books and articles. In terms of volunteer work, I want to help the poor and Mother Earth."

Academic retirement transpired on July 2, 2018—a significant end to my life as full-time Professor, teacher, and researcher—starting a life oriented toward helping others. Academic life had been frustrating, rewarding, anxiety-provoking, eye-opening, sad, epiphanous, and over-all a worthwhile experience. As I write this, a new chapter is unfolding. I want to follow what David Brooks calls climbing the second mountain, or those aspects of life oriented away from selfish behaviors. Even more accurately, my aspiration resonates with what Thomas Merton wrote in his own autobiography, *The Seven Storey Mountain*: to seek a path of faith, a life of simplicity, silence, and contemplation. Perhaps most accurately I want to follow what the author of *The Cloud of Unknowing* called "the lively longing for God." A part of what is driving these changes is a great desire to help others in a more direct way and specifically to help those who appear to need such help. I have always felt blessed and obligated to give back by serving others.

One such case involved my work as a volunteer with Elderhelp, a San Diego organization providing information and personalized services enabling seniors to remain independent and live with dignity in their own homes. In October of 2016, I was assigned to help an Elderhelp client named Shari, a sixty-five-year-old single woman with medium-length, slightly disheveled gray hair and living in the Pacific Beach area of San Diego. She reminded me of someone I had known but could not remember. My initial reaction was one of surprise at how young Shari was. I had assumed that Elderhelp clients were at least eighty or older, housebound, and in need of help grocery shopping. Aside from knee problems that constrained her from getting in and out of a chair easily, Shari could walk well enough, once upright. I was suspicious and uncertain that she needed my help.

That first meeting, Shari wanted to visit Trader Joe's, the hardware store, and Kentucky Fried Chicken—in that order. I was soon engaged with her in an animated conversation while I drove her around. I learned she was very intelligent, had graduated from UCSD as a History major, the same university I worked at, and was still working doing some editing/translation of legal documents. She had a brother who lived in Temecula, California, about an hour's drive north of San Diego. Unfortunately, she did not have a good relationship with him. She also had a sister who lived in Louisiana and visited her occasionally. Shari's cynicism about her work and family took me by surprise, for she exhibited a humorous personality with an edge. I liked her. My visits offered Shari an opportunity to get out of the house, and do her banking and shopping at least twice a month. She and I soon became close. Our meetings, although still under the auspices of Elderhelp, are no longer a volunteer-to-client relationship, but friend-to-friend. After our first meeting, I came away thinking the greatest gift I can give another is my time and attention.

My new heart—mind felt comfortable helping the elderly. I suppose I saw myself more in them than in any other age group. I soon began volunteering for Serving Seniors in 2017, a downtown San Diego center providing a variety of resources to elderly folks at or below the poverty line. At least once a week for the past year and a half I help to serve lunch at the three offerings that occur each day. I was wary the first time I served lunch and nervous when over hundred individuals came in for their meal. Six to eight men and women sit around circular or rectangular tables and get lunch on plastic trays. I stared uneasily at them thinking these healthy and normal-looking seniors did not seem in need. There must be some mistake. It saddened me to think these folks had fallen through the cracks, and yet happy that resources such as Serving Seniors existed. After a few months, I volunteered to teach a class called Brain Fitness for the seniors. The class provided information on how to maintain a healthy brain. The response from those who enrolled was terrific. I have continued teaching it regularly. Word of mouth has spread and I am now being invited to present similar classes at other senior centers.

One morning, it occurred to me that I needed to learn to empathize with folks at the end of their life. This is a time of heightened intensity of feelings. After a bit of research on the Internet, I called the Hospice of the South Coast, an organization created to provide high-quality end-of-life care and bereavement services to terminally ill folks and their families. Hospice trained and assigned me my first client named Greg. Unfortunately, Greg succumbed to his disease soon after my first visit and left me wondering whether I wanted to do this. Not long afterwards, I met Barbara (Bobbie) and her husband, Dave. Bobbie had entered hospice many months prior. She and Dave, both in their late eighties and having lived a full life as a real estate agent and architect, respectively, turned out to be sweet and wonderful individuals, married for close to sixty years. I began visiting them at least once a week and felt that my responsibility was to be present, be a friend, converse, and provide a sense of caring. I quickly learned to bring cookies since Bobbie has a very sweet tooth—something we share in common. Both she and Dave appreciated the efforts of the hospice team and my efforts to check in on them. If there is anything I have learned from this experience, it is to show patience when waiting for death to ring the doorbell.

My growing awareness, because of my recent realization experience, has led me to a strong commitment to helping others. As this awareness has increased, I have found my strong drive to read-especially spiritual books-markedly reduced, although I continue to enjoy reading and am open to new ideas. The motivation to switch from reading to being could not be clearer.

B. Making Thoughts Real

Given the significant changes brought about by the realization I experienced, questions have arisen concerning what the value and meaning of this new life is. How does the new heart—mind fit in with my retirement? How do I integrate this new reality with my old ways of thinking and behaving? And perhaps most important, how do I explain these changes? These questions arose from an understanding predicated on knowing who I am, which arose following my de-identification with the mythologies of me I had created. While this is still an ongoing process, it has led to my understanding that I am more than my body and my biology. My life review has been an ongoing attempt to get at the truth of this nature. Whether as a scientist studying the mind-brain or as a spiritual searcher trying to understand the heart—mind through Zen and Nondualism, the effort has provided some insights into this nature.

My mind-brain, the biological and psychological substrates of who I am, is not only complex but also deceptively complex. Understanding this puzzle required, as a first step, understanding how the self orchestrates the deception. The deception I refer to, as hopefully has become clear by now, is a created self that is more illusion than real, with a set of habitual thoughts, responses, and expectations created to protect the developing organism. This protective reaction to the world creates artificial boundaries and categories, dividing what is an indivisible nature. The mind-brain then organizes the information and thinks of it in terms of separation. The outcome produces the belief in a separate self and a reality external to itself.

One example of the indivisibility and interdependency with the rest of creation is my need for oxygen, which plant life provides. Reciprocally,

I provide carbon dioxide for their survival. Without this interchange of gases, neither plants nor human or animal life would survive.

What explains all these changes I've experienced? I can only make educated guesses. For one, I am convinced that the existence of the virtual me, or created persona, obscured my true nature. But thinking and the created self themselves were not the primary problems, as both are natural consequences of our mind-brain. So, what remains? More likely it begins with the attachment to thoughts and their materialization into a real entity that creates this mental disorder. Reification is the word typically used by psychologists and philosophers to refer to this transmuting of the immaterial by regarding it as a material construct, force, or value. Reification is seen as a psychological process that, like a glue, can bind thought into a constellation of thoughts and brings its reality into being, making the thoughts concrete. It is arguable that a spectrum or the degrees to this process exist, with the most extreme condition being when one reifies, grasps, and decontextualizes to make the cloud solid and real. The self then becomes identified with the reification of the cloud of habits, expectations, and thoughts.

Assuming this happens, then what is the outcome if the identification/reification process is eliminated? Presumably, thoughts would no longer bind. They would not "stick" and become attached to other thoughts, and as a result would quickly vanish. I practice mindfulness exercises, promoting this nonattachment for precisely this reason. What I found after some time doing this is that what remains is the effortless, spontaneous, in-the-moment, self-originating expression of true beingness. This new sense of being I take to be my true nature, which existed prior to the development of individuation, or what we had as children before the development of a theory of mind. I made the mistake of thinking an opening of this new heart—mind would be a return to a primitive, nonconscious, nonfunctional state. Far from it. What we return to is the new heart—mind described earlier, which is valuable in its own beingness.

It is tempting as a scientist to find biological explanations for these insights. It is almost as if by doing so I validate them. I have chosen not to do that and to trust my intuitive insights and not doubt them by resorting to other explanations. Is this short-sighted? I don't think so, for it is far, far more valuable at this point in my life to learn to trust that part of my developing nature. I can foresee that once total trust becomes the natural state, then fanciful explorations of scientific validation would have a different reason for being engaged. I even predict that scientific quests would be more productively expressed.

C. Aftereffects on Academic Work

Twenty-eight years of academic work and inhabiting an academic mindset did not end suddenly on the day of my retirement. There was momentum and inertia of these interests that extend even to the present. My goal is to concentrate on those aspects of life that have become so much more important, so much more valuable, and so much more rewarding. However, academic work still occurs and I spend at least two days a week at the university with colleagues.

My primary collaborator, Dr. Fiza Singh, a Psychiatrist in the Psychiatry Department, agreed to share her lab space with me. Her kindness has allowed me to continue working on projects started prior to my retirement. Nevertheless, I feel a lessening in my interest in science; I am also more convinced than ever of the limits to science and problems with its assumptions. Specific to cognitive neuroscience is the misunderstanding of the relationship between the individual and nature at large. Neuroscience insists on viewing the individual as an isolated organism. This perspective does not give sufficient weight to environmental and extrasomatic influences influencing and changing brain circuits. Without such sensitivity, understanding how the complex machinery of the brain works becomes difficult. Despite all these changes, my appreciation for the complexity and beauty of the mind-brain has not lessened.

CHAPTER SIX
Conclusion

There is a scarcity and fulfillment antagonism
That afflicts the human mind.
The best solution is to quiet the mind,
Through nonjudgmental observation.
And the two shall become
Not-one, not-two but an interactivity.

A. The Scarcity and Fulfillment Mind

After completing this life review, what has become clear is that the events, circumstances, incidents, accidents, hopes, and motivations that made up my life reflect a confluence of rivulets into two larger streams which are now co-joined. I have existed for most of my life in the entanglement of these two streams. From a psychological perspective, the entanglement reveals one stream, what I call a "scarcity mind," in which my mind deals with contradictory feelings, i.e., sadness and happiness, confidence and fear, etc. And it expresses a sense of lacking, of something missing, some vital source that it needs. In the other stream, is what I call a "fulfilled mind." This is a mind expressing a sense of contentment, fulfillment, and joy. From a spiritual perspective, in which I sense I am more than my body and biology, the entanglement manifests as the struggle between my individuality (scarcity mind) and the unity of existence (fulfilled mind). This dynamic antagonism has played out since my birth, creating both problems and infinite possibilities.

My scarcity mind was an outcome of an intellect craving information and lacking satisfaction. This was foundational for my scientific mindset, one in which such dissatisfaction fueled my natural curiosity, my discontent, and my endless desire to do—anything. Such a scarcity mind likely exists in all of us, and dissatisfaction is undoubtedly the driving force behind humanity's technological and scientific revolutions. It has been the basis for a psychological emptiness that I and most of humanity feels during our development. It is an emptiness difficult to fill and can lead to physical and mental disorders. Mostly, the social and psychological environments I created or found myself in fed my scarcity mind. These psychosocial dynamics produced an imbalance which I felt needed correction. Part of the reason for such an imbalance is the unfortunate perception that a fulfilled mind is unmotivated and unproductive and thus unappreciated by society at large. While this is a misattribution of what such a mind construes as important, the point bears further discussion.

My fulfilled mind reflects a genuine experience of true satisfaction and fulfillment. What I call my "realization" is a mind fulfilled by being and expressing mental abundance without much of the accompanying negativity humans exhibit. For me, these experiences were and are beyond conceptual thinking, difficult to discuss, and hence have a spiritual sense to them. I have learned that a fulfilled mind is possible only in quietude—in silence and in grace.

My scarcity mind temporarily obscured my fulfilled mind by feeling balanced for short periods of time until time ran out and dissatisfaction emerged once again. Once aware of this dynamic, I searched for a long-term resolution to such a recurring problem. The best solution I came across, tried and tested for thousands of years, is to quiet the mind through nonjudgmental observation or what I have also called nonattachment exercises. These methods require experiencing what comes up in one's thoughts and avoiding judgmental aspects *vis-à-vis* those thoughts. Without judgment, thoughts will not stick. We will not reify them.

My exploration of Zen and mindfulness meditation allowed me time and space to practice these nonjudgmental exercises over a forty-year period, until an understanding gradually developed that thoughts have no actual solidity. Like clouds in the sky, they are empty of substance. I ceased to identify with my thoughts. Once that process started, I began to experience periods of less and less mind chatter and more and more stillness and quietude. The mind will gradually quiet on its own accord and might even drop off completely. One check on my progress was recognizing how much of what was happening at the moment was of importance. The less I focused on mind chatter, driven primarily by memories, the more real and important the reality of the world became. I also measured progress in the feeling of abundance, a characteristic of all nature. The realization that an apple tree does not produce one apple but an abundance of apples is transformational. The recognition of this abundance principle in life became more and more pronounced. Accompanying these progressions will be a switch from scarcity to fulfilled thinking, with a fulfilled mind being an abundant mind.

When my mind became calm enough, I sensed that the external world was part and parcel of my internal landscape, and I began to understand there is no need to do, only to be. But, to be in the wonderment of life does not mean disengagement from life or passivity in my actions. Just the opposite, for I could sense that what I saw affected what I was. There was actually an intimacy and personalization of my frame of reference calling for involvement with the world. What is typically misunderstood by others is that the values associated with this new awareness differ significantly from those found in the scarcity state. No longer do I value getting ahead for the sake of money or possessions. I now valued helping others. Life moved from a fear-driven, zero-sum game to a joyful and love-driven enjoyment. This new heart—mind exuded an appreciation and grateful-ness for the gift of life. What I needed in life seemed to be always free and available.

B. Streams: Not-One, Not-Two

My life in hindsight appears to have been the work of a greater intelligence, an intelligence both enigmatic and hidden, but now the essence of what I am. What I have done, learned, and practiced have come together fittingly in a song of praise to this universal intelligence or grace. My life review and the ideas expressed within are expressions of such a song. In the course of a lifetime, the universality of the melody has become clear—for it is an idea expressed by Walt Whitman in *Song of Myself* in 1892:

> *I celebrate myself, and sing myself,*
> *And what I assume you shall assume,*
> *For every atom belonging to me as good belongs to you.*

Over a lifetime, I have faced circumstances that could have produced serious consequences, yet I walked away unscathed. These are not unique events to me for many of us have experienced them. A guardian energy hung over my shoulder; an energy I now realize is Life itself. In the long run, this has made living more positive than negative. More joyful than sad. More optimistic than pessimistic. I have enjoyed countless opportu-nities to live a good, full life and to express such energy optimally. Since childhood, my inquisitive mind asked questions and had ready answers to the questions posed by teachers. It has been both a blessing and a curse serving its purpose, like the sword of Mañjuśrī cutting down ignorance and duality. Inquisitiveness has taken me toward my vocation and avoca-tion in science and spirituality. Both pathways reflect the greatest mysteries of all—the play of consciousness as both unity and individuality. They are two sides of the same coin. They reflect Buber's "I am in God and God is in me" or as developed in my story, the antagonism between the scarcity and fulfilled mind, or the mind-brain and the heart—mind.

Looking back on my life, I can see the dance, the antagonism, reflected in the back and forth between two streams of consciousness I've characterized as the scarcity and fulfilled mind. Another visual metaphor for the same thing is the tangled strings of the DNA. In one string or stream, there is me with the inquisitive and natural tendencies of a scientist interested in the material universe. This passion has taken me toward understanding how the mind interacts with biological substrates. The brain became a fascinating and important locus of interaction. However, the goal of this stream of consciousness only became clear in retrospect. Its zigzag nature made its course difficult to, in-the-moment, know the direction or the meaningfulness of its actions. In the second string or stream, I became fascinated by the spiritual nature of being. My spiritual nature recognized the unreality of the mythology of me, the invented persona forming the core of my being. The more my spiritual nature became the focus of exploration, the less real the constructed persona became.

This relationship led to another significant turning point in my life, where the true nature of my spiritual being revealed itself. This point of understanding coincided with the winding down of my career as a scientist. The timely collapse of the two streams into not-one, not-two, but an interactivity served as a resolution to the psychospiritual crisis dogging me throughout. What I understood is that science provided me with the ability to understand truth intellectually by deconstructing or disintegrating the world, especially the psychological and biological me. However, this reductionism or disintegration by itself is not enough. There is a need to integrate and to understand the whole, not just the separate parts. Science attempts to do it but fails—the job is just too big for conventional intellectualism. Spirituality is another name for this process of integration. What one finds and experiences in this path is truth concerning the unity of life and of being. The spiritual eye sees the unity, the relationship between the parts. The job is not too big for this mind's eye.

The paradox is that with discernment, the scientific drive lessens, the need to know for the sake of knowing lessens, and the compulsion to know to manipulate life lessens. And what it leaves at the end is an overwhelming sense of acceptance and appreciation for the beauty, order, disorder, and purpose of life. It is the essence of love, that presence or sense of stillness and unity, that allows things to settle naturally into their own beingness.

Scientific research and teaching are Life's capacity and intention to know itself, a real awakening process. Awakening becomes the mind's surrender of its authority to the heart of awareness. Spirituality then becomes the naturalness of life itself. Many individuals across history have reached a similar conclusion. Ralph Waldo Emerson (1803–1882) reimagined the divine as visible nature, an idea known as Transcendentalism. Baruch de Spinoza (1632–1677), Dutch philosopher and one of the early thinkers of the Enlightenment believed that God is "the sum of the natural and physical laws of the universe and certainly not an individual entity or creator." Even Jesus made a similar connection in the identity between spirit and life when he said, "The words I have spoken to you are spirit and they are life." (John 6:63). Finally, Lao Tzu (fifth or sixth century BC), a Chinese philosopher, writer, and presumed author of the *Tao Te Ching*, considered the founder of philosophical Taoism, spoke a similar truth thousands of years ago when he asked:

Why scurry about looking for the truth?
It vibrates in everything and every not-thing, right off the tip of
your nose.
Can you be still and see it in the mountain? The pine tree? Yourself?
Don't imagine that you'll discover it by accumulating more knowledge.
Knowledge creates doubt, and doubt makes you ravenous for
more knowledge.
You can't get full eating this way.
The wise person dines on something more subtle:
He eats the understanding that the named was born from
the unnamed,
that all being flows from non-being,

that the describable world emanates from an indescribable source.

He finds this subtle truth inside his own self,

and becomes completely content.

So, who can be still and watch the chess game of the world?

The foolish are always making impulsive moves,

but the wise know that victory and defeat are decided by something
more subtle.

They see that something perfect exists before any move is made.

This subtle perfection deteriorates when artificial actions are taken,

So be content not to disturb the peace.

Remain quiet.

Discover the harmony in your own being.

Embrace it.

If you can do this, you will gain everything,

and the world will become healthy again.

If you can't, you will be lost in the shadows forever."

EPILOGUE

In retrospect, the path is clear,
As I look back six decades hence.
I walk in joy the road less travelled,
For It has chosen me.

This life review has convinced me that I am more than my body and my biology. We are all much more than the obvious physical, biological organisms we seem to be. Whatever that superorganism is, I still root it in physicalness. But at its core, it is still a mystery. Yet that mystery is also an experience of awareness and profound stillness holding everything in its bosom. While everything is constantly changing, this holding awareness does not. My story is not only a variation of all other human stories, but one reality, the holding awareness, experiencing life differently through each of us. It is the unity expressing itself individually. From another perspective, our developing awareness is life becoming conscious of itself. This has led me to insights about the true nature of who I am, who the person named Jaime is. To consciously know who I truly am required me to step into my separateness (to embody my separate self) and then transcend it by recognizing its unreality.

The conclusion of this review of my life must answer the questions posed in my Prologue. I recognize that they are answerable, and I'll respond to them one at a time. First, why do "I" as an individual exist? My individuality and unique existence are such powerful experiences I did not question them. They obscure the reality that my story is a story repeated a thousand times. I am not as unique an individual as my ego led me to think. Why does an "I" exist? When I explored this persona, I realized that this entity is only the stories I created and retold over the years. Not that I had no need for such a cover story. Its role as a protective mechanism facing the full storm of life has been valuable. However, while its protective role was necessary when I was young, the need became less and less as I reached adulthood. By that time, the stories had gained a solidity to them, which became my reality and truth. Yet, when I examined them closely, they dissolved. They disappeared like the solidity of a cloud, which—when pierced—is more space than the water molecules forming the cloud.

Like all children, I developed a theory of mind: the ability to distinguish self from others and to know others can think different thoughts than I do. The outcome was my individuation arising from the natural "oneness" of being. Asking what causes individuation leads to a combination of biology and psychology, nature and nurture, including the necessity to know dangers to survive, coupled with stories regarding myself.

Second, if no personal "I" exists or is unnecessary, then what is the remaining experience when the personal mythologies evaporate? What became clear when this piercing of the cloud occurred to me is the experience of oneness, of the unity and continuity of life. I returned to my natural or true sense of being where life recognized itself in me. The recognition that I am life became more real than my own individual experience. Hence, my sense now is that I don't exist so much as an individual. I exist as an expression of the larger beingness of life.

Third, is there a role for me in life? From the above perspective, the question becomes meaningless because the real question is: Whether "there is a role for life itself"? The answer is obvious, given we all live on a planet where life expresses itself in many forms. The question of the meaningfulness of life persists. Granted that humans are but one out of billions of expressions, am I still special? Do I stand out? There is a strong drive, especially in Western cultures, to think this way, and I can make arguments for such uniqueness. From life's perspective, I am no more unique than the bat who echolocates or the eel who senses using electromagnetic fields. Is my difference because of obvious intelligence? Sure, as unique as the large size of dinosaurs who ruled the Earth for millions of years before disappearing. My individual intelligence, combined with all other human intelligences, is leading us to our own demise. In fact, the continuing human actions affecting the Earth and its climate do not seem so smart. Earth and life will continue even if I and others of my race disappear. We, and I in particular, do not have a privileged existence. Life itself does.

From a personal perspective, I came into being with a set of biological and nonbiological predispositions. I inherited several predispositions from my parents. Others came from siblings, teachers, friends, strangers, and circumstances. A few involved biological mechanisms like DNA, while others involved behaviors learned or responses elicited by others. My inquisitive nature reflected a sensitivity to order and the need for it. As life expressed itself through my physical body and mind, the effect resembled the creation of an inimitable tune. Different people produce unique tunes, even if they come from poor Central American countries. Like players tuning their instruments to prepare for a concert, there can be discordant sounds, irritating and uncomfortable when we act alone. The voluminous individual tunes, however, become part of a grander and exquisite symphony in coordination.

Life maximized and fine-tuned my song by creating conditions exposing me to the true nature of my individual notes. Life also plays the role of a conductor. What I saw as negative events, sacrifices, unmet needs, etc. were part of the complex dynamics of the refinement process. Thus, all positive and negative circumstances in my life are examples of complex ongoing refinement.

Refinement for me occurred when my Uncle Joe moved to the United States and willingly offered me the prospect of a better life. The process continued when my Mom sacrificed her attachment to the young me or when I married two wonderful people, Liz and Jane, and ended up being divorced by one. More refinement happened during my service in the military and when I met friends who helped and guided me. Fine-tuning came from my family's tragic car accident and from taking part in the formation of the Department of Cognitive Science. Kindergarten, grade, middle and high school, college, and university are institutions where I exposed my little made-up self to the fire of reality. Or, when Zen masters and guardian angels like my friend Pablo and teacher Joko performed a similar task. Likewise, I feel I have an inherent obligation to take part in life—to provide my individual tune to the grand symphony. I find pleasure in giving back to life, to family, to children, to friends, to strangers and organizations. I give back my time, energy, advice/counsel, and especially affection. I have found this obligation in my teaching, environmental mindset, volunteerism, and poetry writing. Those actions, all oriented toward others, have convinced me life is meaningful for no other reason than the fact that love and grace exist.

Fourth, is it important what "I" do? Within a small and localized space, my actions appear important. From the larger perspective, they don't. Yet, the sense of life caring whether I matter is answered by the recurring patterns in my life, which make up a resounding "yes." Caring started with living in a happy and loving atmosphere, with family, teachers, friends, and strangers who showed me loving kindness. A loving environment created the circumstances and the recurring feeling that forces outside of my control can protect me from unexpected occurrences able to silence my tune. My recurring sense is one of a larger unity protecting and caring for my welfare—and still doing so. Skeptics will pose the question, "Why then do bad things happen to good people?" To answer such a question, I would need to know the goal of creation, which is beyond my individual capacity.

Fifth, is the fact that "I" ended up as a researcher studying the mind-brain meaningful? Looking back, my destiny seems preordained and predictable. My nature, interests, exposure to events and people, expectations, and opportunities created a river of consciousness in which I traveled to an inevitable encounter. This is not so surprising from the larger perspective of life which makes possible the creation of disturbances in the stream and rerouting of the flow affecting what appears inevitable. These are worthwhile metaphysical issues to consider, although beyond this story.

Sixth, are these even worthwhile questions to ask? My perspective may not be your perspective. My optimistic sense is that wrestling with the same questions, especially the question of who we are, can bring us to an agreement. What is clear from reviewing my life is what a fortunate affair my life has been. Many personalities and circumstances appeared during my time on Earth to help, care for, nurture, challenge, oppose, reward, guide, trick, support, question, and teach me what I needed to learn. The multiplicity of faces and events converge into a unified stream. Life itself has been a wonderful teacher, never making the task too difficult to learn. The pounding of life experiences has smoothed out the rough edges, exploded the mythologies of me, and provided a glimpse of what is real. Like the writer of *The Cloud of Unknowing* makes clear, there are transformations occurring in knowing the truth. One is the transformation from thoughts of *what I am* to the awareness *that I am and God is*. The final step is to drop even such awareness. What is left? What I am is life as it is.

One final question raised is: How long it might take you, the reader, to reach a similar understanding or have a similar experience? What can you do to get there? I would say this is directly proportional to the solidity of your virtual self. It is possible to accept this perspective and let go of the virtual self in the blink of an eye and immediately reach the freedom of being. More realistically, it will take time, as it did for me, to recognize the problem, address it, practice letting go, realize the futility of the search and of the practice, and then truly let go. Whether the process is slow or fast, at the end, when it is clear what you have gone through, you will have a good laugh, for you realized you are always at that point and have always been the "new" heart—mind. I am grateful to have lived such a joyful life experience. May you find some part of your story in mine. In the end, I would like my epitaph to read: "Life lived fully and well in Jaime."

As I complete my story in 2019, Honduras, the country of my origin, has been in the news a great deal. In the early 1960s, when I first arrived in the United States, few people knew Central America and Honduras even less so. Today, immigration from that part of the world, which finds itself in turmoil, has exploded and become a political liability. Its newsworthiness has turned the story into an opportunity for demagogue politicians to use the problem as a wedge issue. Daily, news anchors report caravan after caravan of hundreds, if not thousands, of people moving through Mexico to the United States. These demagogues have created a distorted image of the men, women, and children who are making the difficult trek. They portray them as criminals, rapists, and terrorists, not as individuals escaping an untenable situation and searching for a better life. Therefore, lacking empathy and compassion, the only option for the U.S. natives is to stop this migration at any cost.

Meanwhile, Hondurans are helpless, caught in a socioeconomic and political turmoil at home where they live in a world in which drugs are the economic engine of survival. They face the unenviable choice of leaving or staying and if they stay then being sucked into a hellish life. The smart ones leave, primarily to the United States, the land of plenty and of opportunity. Thus, the prospect of a better and more normal life creates an unstoppable motivation. I did not leave Honduras under such unfortunate circumstances, but left in search of a better education.

I found my way legally into the United States, found the education, and became a scientist and teacher. Thus, a third reason for writing this life review is to present a view of Honduras from the perspective of a native son who emigrated to the United States, and to show that not all those who emigrate are bad people. Most resemble refugees in other parts of the planet whose only goal is to make the best of the gift of life granted to them. When given those opportunities, it is possible for the benefits to sometimes outweigh the costs.